Note on Pronunciation

Sanskrit words have been rendered into English in the form most convenient for the public. Thus the letter sometimes presented by scholars as ś is given as sh, and the nasals sometimes presented as ṁ are given as n or m, as they are pronounced in Sanskrit. Vowels: ā is as in father, ī as ee, ū as oo, e as in prey, ai as in aisle, au as in how. In Chinese words, the mark ' indicates that the preceding letter is to be sounded exactly as in English. Otherwise the letters p, t, k, ch, and ts are somewhat sonant, near b, d, g, j, and dz. Ih is as ee, ieh as i-ay, eh as er, en as un, and ong as ung. Jn (in jnana prajna, etc.) has about the sound of gny, but this varies a little in different provinces.

E. W.

A

Abstractions. An example of the Zenist avoidance of abstractions is:
When the Zen Master Tokusan became enlightened, he said, 'All our
understanding of the abstractions of philosophy is like a hair in space.'
Another, when the idea of difficulty was brought up in the matter of
solving a certain problem, remarked, 'It is like a mosquito trying to
bite into an iron bull.'

A certain logician, a non-Zenist, hearing of these, questioned: 'Is
this just a method of avoiding the conclusion in a syllogism, and an
insistence entirely on the adequacy of the premises only, based upon
the senses?' The answer that the premises or perceptions require no
thought was challenged as itself a thought, but this was denied on the
ground that it referred only to the notion of perception without
thought. The two examples given above show that the Zenist has no
objection to analogy, when it serves to express an experience, not to
make a comparison.

Ālaya. This word means a house, or rather a home, which is in turn a
place where all the valued things for use by us are kept and among
which we dwell. It came to mean also the spiritual storehouse of all
the potentialities of life, which is to be regarded as our true home, and
also as our ultimate destination.

There is naturalness, not mere mysticism, in this idea, because we
see that life in Nature is something *sui generis*, in no way a reflex
from the operations of 'dead matter'. The distinctive point about
life in Nature is not so much that it responds to contacts of environment as that it is conscious. If all the complicated actions of the mind
were in fact only reactions (no matter how complicated) and life were
nothing but a collection or collocation of such reflexes, there would
have been no occasion for the rising of consciousness in the process of
the organic development of life. This remark is entirely without
prejudice to (or against) the Oriental belief that right down to and in
the mineral forms in Nature there is some degree of consciousness
and voluntary life.

So ālaya is the infinitely existent self-nature present as potential in
all living beings, and is that which Buddha experienced directly (not
through reasoning such as is given in this note on ālaya) in full

consciousness at the time of his illumination. Zenists hold that this is possible for everybody.

Amitābha. Literally, immortal light. Sometimes called Amitāyus, immortal life. Also Amida. Avalokiteshwara is called the 'Spiritual son' of Amitābha. Manjushri is another aspect of divinity, expressing wisdom. These forms of divinity are often depicted in Zen mōnasteries, sometimes in the form of statues, but the Zenists do not look for help from them, as the followers of the Pure Land Sect do, although they salute them with bows and reverence.

Anatta. The anatta or anātmā doctrine taught by Buddha, to which most Buddhists, including Zenists, subscribe, is briefly the 'not self' idea of man's true nature. This is not to be confused with the 'not-self' expression used in Hindu philosophies. It means that the true nature of man is not conceivable by the human mind, because that mind knows only objects, and therefore what men call 'myself' is not in any respect themselves. Buddha taught that even with the best of understanding this 'myself' is only a bundle of five tendencies, called skandhas (branches), including form, emotions, perceptive faculties, tendencies or habits of character, and mental ability or discrimination, including the idea of oneself as an entity among other entities.

In Hinduism the ātman is the Self, and the anātman is the not-self, that is, all the objective things in the world, which are 'not-self', and the great aim is to recognize the Self, and seek and serve it. With them, ahankāra (the I-maker), Buddhi (the higher intelligence) and manas (the logical intelligence), together with all compounds of the five elements (bodies composed of earth, water, heat, air and sky-matter) are the not-self, and the ātman beyond all those is the Self, the real dehin (owner of the body).

Although Buddha said that the idea of such a dehin as an entity was wrong, he nevertheless held to the reincarnation of the false 'self', the set of skandhas, subject to constant change until the Truth replaced it, when the skandhas would be ready to fall apart (would cease to make time) and only the Truth would *be*, in its own way or suchness. Buddhist poets have allowed themselves expressions such as 'The dewdrop slips into the shining sea,' and 'The Universe grows I,' but even these, and indeed all concepts bred in the mind of man, must be wrong. At least they indicate, however, that the very idea of a permanent separate entity is wrong and stands in the way of Truth and Illumination. The most enlightened Hindus held thē same view as Buddha in this matter, as is well expounded in Chapter 13 of the *Bhagavad Gitā*, where the Lord enumerates the eight constituents of man (the five elements and ahankāra-buddhi-manas, the latter three being comprised in the modern term 'the mind' in its most comprehensive sense), and states that all eight must be transcended.

Buddha was a reformer, fighting against both scholarly and worldly errors, including social castes and religious creeds. Whatever the reality may be, which is discovered at 'illumination', the thorough-going Zenist Buddhist will allow himself only the idea of its own Thatness or Suchness (tathatā), which is also a void (shūnyatā) or emptiness of all conceivable things or ideas.

The doctrine of anatta (non-ātmā) is common to both Mahāyāna and Theravāda (Hīnāyāna) schools of Buddhism.

Angya. This word means a pilgrimage on foot, and applies to the novice who wishes to join a monastery. His conventional dress includes a wide bamboo rain-hat, white cotton leggings, straw sandals and a satchel containing such things as his razor, bowls, books, etc. Such a journey is beautifully described in a long poem called *The Song of Angya*, composed by Funyo Zensho in the early Sung Dynasty.

On arrival at the monastery, the pilgrim will present his letter of introduction, if he has one, and then wait in the entrance court for several days until admission. On admission he is on probation for another short period before being advanced into the meditation hall, where he bows before the shrine or statue and then is introduced to the brethren.

It is to be taken into account that the pilgrimage is valuable in itself. The personal and bodily difficulties faced and overcome, including inclement weather, are awakening and strengthening on one side, while the varying beauties of Nature and the constant meeting with varied persons and human activities are culturally beneficial on the other. It may be that on the pilgrimage, and not in the visit with a Zen Master, the Satori will come, but the pilgrim must on no account expect it in either case.

An-Shih-kao. First advocate of the Ch'an or meditation doctrine in China, about A.D. 150.

Anuttara-samyak-sambodhi. This is a statement about the experience of illumination by a Buddha. Anuttara means that it has nothing beyond (is the ultimate); samyak, correct; sambodhi, complete knowing. This does not refer to the highest of a series of experiences, but to what is beyond all categories and relativity. It is *the* Truth, reachable by meditation (dhyāna or Zen).

Arhat. A term much used by Buddha, but not by Zenists. It means 'ready', and was applied only to certain of his followers. The qualifications of the Arhat may be seen by reference to what Buddha called the ten fetters – fetters being defects of character which obstruct the true or essential realization. The first five fetters are (1) the delusion of the personal self, which is the thoughtless acceptance of the notion of oneself as body and mind, (2) doubt about the efficacy of

9

the good life, (3) dependence upon ceremonies, (4) emotional desires, (5) emotional aversions. It is easy to see in these five the following of old unphilosophical mental habits.

These automatic responses being overcome, the disciple on the Path is ready (arhat) to face and overcome (6–7) the desire for life in form and formless life, (8) spiritual pride, (9) the notion of oneself as entity, and (10) ignorance of the nature of the essential self. Although the Zenists do not follow this classification, they, in following the 'direct method', are thereby at work overcoming the last five.

Artist and Picture. A simile which has been used to exemplify the relation between the higher self, or the character of a man (his will, love and thought), and his lower self, composed of his body and his habits of emotion and thought, including his memory. The 'lower self' does not cause the improvements to the 'higher self', which are due to his own thought, love and will, though it provides material or data for working upon. Thus in Buddhism the higher self is the artist and the lower self the picture. In each life or incarnation, karma re-presents the artist with the work of his past, while the artist reappears also modified by his past efforts. Thus the artist learns not to confuse himself with his picture, the lower self, on which it is his business now to work, rather than upon the 'pictures' of others. Zen, however, goes a step further than this simile, and sets the artist to work upon the 'higher self', to reject even it as 'myself', and to seek the Buddha-nature of Buddha-mind beyond it.

Artistry. The art of Japan has taken forms which indicate influence by Zen. Perhaps most typical is the shrine of beauty which is found in every good home. On a section of the wall there will be one scroll picture (kakemono) and perhaps one flower in a simple vase on a small table or stool or shelf.

The one flower is probably the most indicative feature of the display. Man can naturally enjoy one flower without strain, and from it can obtain all the loving union which is the heart of the sense of beauty that is possible for him without strain and its consequent breach of harmonious association. A bouquet is aggressive and overwhelming, stimulating perhaps, but demanding, and requiring that coping which drains the man while increasing his power.

The picture will be changed from time to time; there is a stock of them somewhere out of sight. A quantity of pictures causes distraction. On the other hand, a long continuance of one leads to inattention, since life is movement, not staticness.

In painting, it is remembered that painting is only suggestion, that a picture of a cow does not present a cow, and does not represent a cow except to one educated to that conventionality. Similarly alphabets do not represent sounds, but are conventional. The logical conclusion of this view of representation by the painting art is that the minimum of representation with the maximum of impressiveness is most 'speaking' for the man unconventionalized to an art system. This is naturalness. And this we find in Japanese art, in the brush strokes with their deepenings and fadings, their broadenings and narrowings, their directionings or pointings, and their spacings so indicative of known relationships requiring no thought. It is all akin to the one-flower decor.

The skill required for painting (Sumiye) aims at producing a similar effect. The materials required are prepared with the greatest care. The paper is very thin, and quickly absorbs the ink, so that the artist must make his stroke in one movement, quite spontaneously, for there can be no alterations afterwards. The ink is made of a mixture of soot and glue, and is always black, though it can be put on the paper with dense blackness or lightly. The brush is made from the hair of a sheep or a badger, which holds plenty of ink; and is mounted in a bamboo handle, and shaped to a sharp point. The artist uses it with a free movement without resting the arm or hand on anything. This conduces to the expression of inspiration, resulting in appropriate directions, pressures, depths, etc.

Very closely related to this is Japanese and Chinese calligraphy. Thus, in reading an author's work in his own calligraphy one receives impressions of his feelings as well as the ideas he seeks to convey. As the same kind of brush and paper are used in Sumiye, the same effect of spontaneity appears in the form and thickness of the various strokes.

Arts of Zen. The zenic influence in art involves a replacement of restless detail by quietness, which is the chief 'action' in deep meditation. This is affected by the presentation of the space motive.

In painting, the leaving of portions blank by the placing of only the very necessary strokes on paper, 'leaving the open space to be filled in by the mind', as the expression is, does not set the mind thinking (which is restless) but causes it to poise itself on what it knows (which is quiet or tranquil). This is the discovery that the observer makes when he observes the effect of Zen art in his own mind. It is not that the discovery of this effect is important; it is the effect itself that is so.

It is important that there be some lines. The paper is not to be blank all over, for the reason that in life the mind only becomes aware of the space when it is suggested not by the absence of objects but by the cessation or stoppage (nirodha) of them. For example, a triangle is not properly bounded by three lines, but by three *edges* where the triangle stops. To illustrate this one may cut out a triangle in cardboard or paper, and then hold it up.

It is just the same in the poetry of Zen (haiku, *q.v.*). When the

11

sketchy verse ends, 'The frog jumps into the pond; plop,' one becomes by that aware of a new richness of silence or quietude – not that one *thinks* about it, for thinking about it spoils the effect. One knows it, not thinks about it.

The experience is the richer in both cases – the sumi (painting) and the haiku (poetry) – if the observer has previously found the *mood* of it, in some earlier happy experience of it, arising for the first time in a proper approach. Afterwards the mood can be voluntary. It is thus in the art of meditation. There is an unseen science behind it, which teaches the value of contemplation (in which there is no thinking) and which in fact is samādhi, the rich depth of meditation beyond the thinking phase of it. Even in ordinary poetry (if one may use such an irreverent expression about poetry), the pauses induce this poise, however brief and however unobserved as such, from time to time. That is why an idea expressed in poetry enriches us much more than the same expressed in prose.

The same zenic effect is to be seen in landscaping, such as that in the Ryoanji monastery garden near Kyoto. In that there is an arrangement of certain rocks placed in carefully raked white sand. It is not that the sand is there for our inspection; the rocks are. These may if one likes be given a meaning and be a language for us, but the so carefully unvariegated sand becomes filled for us with the tranquillity of our own deep knowledge, not thought, not even perception. It is just the opposite of what happens when one reads meanings into a confused litter of clouds or wet tea-leaves, or a clutter of chaotic designs, searching as it were for something pleasing and finding (or not finding) one beauty after another.

A good lawn evenly and closely mown, set off with a few suitable plants and flowers, can have a somewhat similar effect to that of the rock garden – but not when there are masses of plants and flowers, however beautiful they may be when taken in smaller doses and without too much mixing together. One can wander in a mixed garden and enjoy it with benefit, but that is not the way of Zen, though there can be in it rich zenic moments when one really views one flower, or something, being caught and held poised by its beauty.

It is the same with skill in actions as with arts, for the sight. The Zen method (upāya) has led in Japan to the skill of judo, for which we have no proper translation in English. The nearest term is perhaps wrestling. But what happens in fact in the situations that arise is the same no-thought – the body is allowed its own wisdom and is completely free from mental driving or direction. In those circumstances its falling or rolling is a completion of natural action, like a willow tree that bends in the wind instead of shuddering and perhaps breaking, and afterwards restores itself not by recovery but by the completion of its own natural action.

There was once a man standing on a chair, placing a light bulb in a ceiling socket. Somehow the bulb slipped from his hand. With unconscious perfection of movement, in both speed and accuracy, he in one motion of good balance bent down and caught the bulb below the level of the chair seat as it was falling, then in one continuous movement was up again with the bulb in his hand at the socket. He says it was an unexpected and most wonderful experience, and he can remember perfectly how his body felt, and indeed can induce himself or rather release himself into the same mood at any time by the memory of the feeling of it. Relaxation is too formal a name for this. It is rather the spontaneous wisdom of the body in something perfectly learned in course of natural adaptation. It is something that cannot be thought of but can be enjoyed in consciousness when thought lets go.

No doubt it is in the same mood and with the same absence of 'I am doing this' that the marvellous skill of Zen archery is attained, or rather that the archery is done with hand, arm and eye in one flowing motion in which there are no decisions.

In some of the Zen arts there seems to be much formalism. In the 'No' drama, for example, the characters are formally and elaborately dressed, and they make motions sometimes suddenly arrested in unnatural poise and speak in an uncanny or sepulchral voice. These characters are, so to say, the rocks in the rock-garden, or they are the ideas in the poetry. They tell the story which is the theme of the play, but the unusual stoppings and startings and utterances – so different from ordinary prosy life – create in the mind of the observer the same zenic poises as occur in poetry or in landscape gardening, where thinking stops and knowing fills the gap, experiencing the emphasis of the story in a way richly new.

In this play the sounds – now the flows and now the clackings, now the flute notes and drums and sharp cries, and now the flow again – all call up the moods of the story in the succession that the story requires. One knows the story beforehand, such as that of the girl who treated so hardly the men who came to court her. There was one whom she specially wanted, but even for him she could not abate her proud cruelty. Though he had to come from a long distance, she insisted that he do so on a hundred nights before she would grant her favours. He died on the hundredth day, and the story then depicts the rest of the life of the woman, lamenting, broken down and crazed in age.

House-decoration – or rather decor – must also be mentioned. Already the flower and the picture (kakemono), in their special place or shrine, have been alluded to, and in connection with them the living restfulness of the 'room'. Is this not what makes the difference between a house and a home? And even in the West, where homes often contain many well-loved treasures, is it not that these, if genuinely loved, speak only of deep-seated knowledge, and not of inquiry and search?

Flower-arrangement? Here, it seems, are quite a few flowers and a statuette, perhaps, or a miniature tree, assembled in or on one vase or jar-garden; the whole to remind us of – something. And somehow these must form one peaceful unit, and speak of a quietness, which can also be known in nature, where water and earth and clouds and sky meet, each being itself, in companionship without molestation.

And so, when we hear, 'Become the bamboo,' or 'Become the bird' – Yes, but must it not be without intention, and something like a dewdrop slipping into a not-too-shining sea?

Asanga. See under Mahāyāna.

Asceticism. Zen practice does not approve of asceticism, but of naturalness. This, on the other hand, does not mean indulgence. It means a sane mind in a healthy body. It involves, for example, eating to live, not living to eat. It involves the choosing of pleasure in bodily affairs, and the avoidance of pain, but not the *pursuit* of pleasure. It recognizes the naturalness of pleasure for the stimulation of the body, but it also recognizes the naturalness of the mind's judgement of naturalness, as being the governor of the desires for sentient pleasure, as knowing when to encourage pleasure, and where to limit it. It recognizes also that, as regards the body, the pleasure of health (which goes with naturalness) is greater than the pleasurable excitement of over-indulgence, or of any indulgence which is not required for the welfare or health of the body.

It was with this in view that celibacy was prescribed for the monks who had retired from the business of life for the purpose of learning, teaching and meditating. It was understood that in this matter of the using up of bodily energies for the 'welfare of another' (that is, for the production of a further generation in the form of offspring) was both unjustified indulgence and waste in the case of the monks and nuns. In their case this abstention was not supposed to involve a terrible emotional struggle, because the understanding of naturalness by the mind would in itself quieten the impulses of past habits and residues of impulse, especially when the individual's greatest interest in life was in the direction of zenic meditation.

This is quite in accordance with Buddhism in general, as is seen in the story of Gautama's search for truth, which ultimately led to his enlightenment by which he visited all the great hatha yogis in his area, and practised their methods to such an extent that he became very emaciated. One day he was found in a swooning condition by a kind housewife, who persuaded him to drink some milk which she brought. Common sense then showed him where proper attention to the body was natural and beneficial, and not long afterwards he attained illumination under the bo-tree at Budh-Gayā. In connection with this event Edwin Arnold, in his *Light of Asia*, quoted the following verse:

> The string o'erstretched breaks, and the music flies;
> The string o'erslack is dumb, and the music dies;
> Tune us the sitar neither low nor high.

Ascription. In Sanskrit, adhyāsa. This word gives a clue to the nature of both Hindu and Buddhist – and especially zenic – meditation. It shows also their similarity in both method and purpose, for in both cases ascription in meditation is to be avoided. One must *not* ascribe to the thing seen a resemblance to something seen before. This is for two reasons: (1) ascription diverts the attention from the object to some extent, since when you say the lion is like a big cat you give some of your attention to the memory of a cat or cats, and your direct observation of the lion is to that extent diminished, or it is diverted from the whole lion to those parts of it in which it resembles a cat, and (2) your desire to know is in some degree assuaged and you are comforted or eased, so that your alertness is diminished. It happens in nature: the animal seeing a new thing is alert – even frightened until it recognizes the object, not necessarily as a specific object, but as like something which has not hurt it before.

But contrary to all this, the real purpose in meditation is to take into consciousness what one has missed before, either in form or in quality.

When in the exercise for concentration one advises, 'First select an object of concentration, and then think of everything else you can without losing sight of it,' the purpose is to keep on returning to the object by your will, and thus to increase the power – instinctive power of control over thoughts and desires. When the zenic pilgrim walks from temple to temple and Master to Master with his question or questions, and the Master responds with a koan (*q.v.*), and the pilgrim meditates on the koan and goes on to another Master, and so on, he is developing the will-power by which some day his old desires and thoughts will no longer deflect his perception, and then – suddenly – he will see his truth and see it whole.

This is not learning from a Master, but learning to see without bar or wall. It is the opposite of philosophy which is 'another story'.

Ashwaghosha. Indian Buddhist of about A.D. 100, who promoted the doctrine of tathatā (thusness or suchness), which later became very prominent in Zen Buddhism. In Ashwaghosha's famous work *The Awakening of Faith* (*q.v.*) he took up the doctrine of ālaya (ālaya-vijnāna). Ālaya means a home, so consciousness must be known in its own home, or as of its own suchness.

This became a doctrine of the Yogāchāra School, which was started by Asanga and Vasubandhu, in India. Ashwaghosha made ālaya very metaphysical, and having its own 'suchness'. The word bhūta-tathatā was used, which may be translated as 'suchness of actuality', or 'suchness of being'. This led many into the idea of it as a mystical reality, and thus Yogāchāra came to be called the Idealistic School of Mahāyāna (*q.v.*). The strict Zenists, however, would not have this idealism, which tends to make the suchness of the true Buddha-mind a sort of storehouse (ālaya) of all possibilities of life, subject to partial expression (and therefore partial occlusion) in or as various forms or bodies (kāya). They held, it appears, that the Buddha-mind must be sought not only without thought of any such things, but also without the thought of it even as a metaphysical reality.

Some think that this position of the Zenists arose not from Indian reasoning, but from the nature of the Chinese mind, as concerning itself with factual experience rather than with reasoning, which involves comparison and judgement. A Vedantist of India would express the same idea by saying it was important to them *not* to fall into adhyāsa (ascription of something known before) when facing a new fact or idea. Since reasoning involves comparing what is now seen with something previously known, it is considered by both Vedantists and Zenists as not conducive to the discovery of the true self (ātman) or the Buddha-mind. If, however, that Buddha-mind is already with us from the beginning, as both Schools hold, then it might be argued that it is that in us which pushes us (who are really fundamentally itself, though by thought confusing ourselves with personal identity) up to the desire for it, or in other words appears in us as an undefined spiritual hunger (as natural as bodily hunger) which is also the source of our natural unsatisfaction with every other gain, that is, of what has been called our 'divine discontent'.

Inasmuch as Ashwaghosha taught that one should aim at identification with the true principle of Mahāyāna by intuition, he can rightly be called a forerunner of Zen.

Avalokiteshwara. Ishwara means Lord, and avalokita looked at or seen. He is the principal Bodhisattwa of the Buddhist pantheon, according to the Lotus Sūtra, which in its 25th Chapter deals with his many transformations. In male form in Chinese he is called Kwan-shai-yin, and in female form Kwan-yin (Kwannon in Japanese), aften alluded to as 'Goddess of Mercy'.

Avatanshaka Sūtra. A Sanskrit scripture of the Mahāyāna Sect in India which became the chief text of the Hua-yen (in Japanese, Kegon) school. One portion of this work is entitled the Gānda-vyūha (*q.v.*). The principal doctrine of the sūtra is that of the Law-nature (dharma-dhātu) of the universe, which in modern terms means that all objects and energies are under law, especially that of causation, on account of which all things are co-existent and interdependent. This implies that there is One Principle present in each of the many, or in each particular. One of its teachings that had much appeal was that fundamentally there is no number – 'neither one nor two'. (See under Number.) In India this sūtra was chief among the scriptures of Mahāyāna Buddhism (*q.v.*) and was very much valued by Bodhidharma and his Zenist followers.

It was not, of course, that the Zenists based themselves on the Sūtra, but that the Sūtra considerably supported their findings, for Zen was not even in the early days involved in philosophy, nor dependent upon ideas at all.

Awakening of Faith. There was a Sanskrit Buddhist Scripture named *Shraddhotpāda*, which was translated into Chinese and then lost. Its author was an Indian Buddhist named Ashwaghosha (*q.v.*). It is now well-known in English under the title *Awakening of Faith*, but obviously the Birth of Faith would have been better, because *utpāda*, the second half of the compound word, means birth or upmoving. Besides, the earlier portion of the Scripture gives reasons for faith, based upon observation of life and birth and death. Only afterwards it proceeds to generalization and finally to the seeking of intuition through faith rather than by thinking.

The remarkable beauty of this text in Chinese is credited mainly to the great Chinese philosopher Chih-i, who assisted Paramārtha to translate it from Sanskrit in A.D. 557.

B

Bankei (1622–93). Writer of Zen poems, who used simple words for the convenience of the public.

Basho Yesei. In Chinese, Pa-chio Hui-ch'ing. A famous writer of Zen poems. (See under Haiku.)

Baso. In Chinese, Ma-tsu (*q.v.*).

Bird's Path, The. To tread the bird's path is an expression in Zen resembling 'living on the wing', instead of with attachment or clinging to particular objects. The idea is to live without a track, like a bird flying in the air, but this must not be mistaken for a goal, as it is only a way of release from a particular form of bondage, and will itself be transcended, so that no negation of unmovingness may tend to be included.

Bodhi. Wisdom, in the sense of enlightenment. It is not accumulated knowledge, is not attainment, is not something found, but is realization of the essential truth.

Bodhidharma (470–543). An Indian Buddhist who went to China, and there formally established the Buddha-Mind School, called also Ch'an and later, in Japan, Zen. His date is generally given as A.D. 520, but some maintain that it occurred in the Liu Sung period, between 420 and 479. He was twenty-eighth in line of the Patriarchs of Zen in India, and carried the Zen method to China, which already had received other forms of Buddhism even as far back as the second century B.C. The Emperor Wu-ti, of the Liang dynasty, an ardent Buddhist, who built and supported many monasteries and temples, received Bodhidharma at his capital Kenko or Chien K'ang (now Nanking) and asked him to define the chief principle of Buddhism. The Emperor was much disturbed and dissatisfied upon receiving as reply only, 'Vast emptiness.'

Bodhidharma then retired to the Shorin (Shao-lin) temple on the Wu-tai Mountain in Honan, and meditated there for nine years facing a wall, as some say, or like a wall, as others have put it. On this subject of wall-contemplation (pi-kuan) Bodhidharma spoke as follows in teaching his disciple and successor Hui-ko (Eka), according

18

to the *Records of the Transmission of the Lamp*: 'When your mind is like a straight-standing wall you may enter into the Path.' There is a story, however, that he sat cross-legged in meditation for nine years in a cave facing a tall cliff called Shoshitsu opposite the temple, without speaking to any of the visitors.

Afterwards he became the founder and first Patriarch of the strict school of Ch'an (Zen), which grew greatly up to the time of its greatest exponent, the Sixth Patriarch, Hui-neng, and became by the end of the Ming Dynasty (1368–1644) the main form of Buddhism in China. Bodhidharma's disciples followed a very ascetic regime.

The Zen movement advanced very rapidly all over China, so that in the T'ang Dynasty (618–906) there were many monasteries, which were centres of education. The Emperors had a high regard for the Zen Masters, and used to invite them to give sermons at court. And so it went on until about A.D. 1300, Zen advancing and the other forms of Buddhism gradually declining, especially, it seems, because it suited the Chinese mind better than the other Schools of Buddhism.

In China Bodhidharma had the name Pu-ti-ta-mo, and in Japan he was called Daruma. His movement acquired the name of the Lanka school also, because he and his school based their teaching on the Lankāvatāra Sūtra. His message to China was summarized in the following verse:

> A special transmission outside the scriptures;
> No dependence upon words and letters;
> Direct pointing at the soul of man;
> Seeing into one's own nature and attainment of Buddhahood.

The immediate successor of Bodhidharma was Hui-ko (in Chinese) or Eka (in Japanese). He was the first Patriarch of Chinese nationality, and author of the following verse, which expressed his understanding of Zen:

> From the seed bed
> Flowers rise,
> Yet there is no seed,
> Nor are there flowers.

Bodhidharma received his name in India from his teacher Panyata, who called him so because of his great knowledge of the Law (dharma or dhamma) or Truth (Bodhi) taught by Buddha. He was originally a kshatriya, son of a king, and became an arhat.

Bodhisattwas. Those followers of Buddha who have reached the point of illumination and have decided not to retire into nirvāna, but to continue in incarnation to help other living beings until all are free. Many Buddhists of the Mahāyāna schools follow this ideal rather than that of the arhat (*q.v.*) and many of them repeat the Bodhisattwa-vow regularly, in anticipation of their future freedom.

The term is composed of bodhi (perfect wisdom or prajñā) and sattwa (an intelligent being whose actions make for harmony). It therefore brings in the principle of karuna or kindness, or love, which is philosophically the experience of unity with others, or, as an endeavour is the practice of unity.

Zenists, however, do not usually make use of the idea, for they do not predicate that prajñā or bodhi or realization implies any thought or act of renunciation, since nirvāna is absolutely indefinable. It could be said that this outlook and effort involves 'relinquishment of the idea of the future' as well as of the past and the present, as stated by the Zen Master Huang-po, also called Hsi-yun, and also Obaku.

Bodhisattwa Vow, The. In the Soto sect, and among many Mahāyānists, there is an oft-repeated vow to remain in the sansāra (*q.v.*) until all beings are free. This should free the aspirant from the desire to be free – which he can never be except by giving up the mental definition of himself, the 'self-image', the sansāric self. 'Whoso loseth his life shall find it, even to the life eternal,' is true in this connection. The losing of that separate life is complete unselfishness, but that is not '*I* am unselfish.' (See under the Soto Sect.) In old Hindu yoga, the desire to avoid or escape is regarded as just as binding as the desire to possess and to hold. That school then advocates the giving up of planning for self (called sankalpa), and the living of a life of action which is entirely motivated by response to the behests of past karma, or the living of that goodness in which every act and thought and word is for the benefit of others and so (as it happens) cancels out some of the stored karma which contains the causes of his now being 'in a body' and 'in an environment'. Yet there must not be this *reason* for the goodness; it must be pure.

Body, the Dense. Many scriptures allude to the body as a combination of four or five 'elements' (earth, water, fire, air and ether – ākāsha, literally sky-matter), and therefore subject to destruction. This is agreeable to Zenists, as well as all other sects.

Bokuju Dosho. In Chinese, Mu-chou. A senior disciple of Rinzai under Obaku, and teacher of Ummon.

Bombu Zen. Just ordinary meditation, with or without philosophic or religious purpose, sometimes only for the good of the mind or of the body. It benefits the mind just as physical exercise benefits the body. It is included within the term mushinjo.

Brick, Story of the. One day Ma-tsu, while still a pupil under the Master Huai-jang, was asked why he sat so very much in meditation. Ma-tsu replied that it was for the purpose of becoming a Buddha. The Master then started rubbing a brick very hard. It was now Ma-tsu's turn to ask a question. 'Why,' he inquired, 'do you rub that brick?' 'To make a mirror,' replied Huai-jang. 'But surely, sir,' protested Ma-tsu, 'no amount of polishing will make a brick into a mirror.' 'And so also,' returned the Master, 'no amount of sitting cross-legged will make you into a Buddha.'

This at first sight seems to dispense with Zen (meditation) altogether, but further on in the conversation it becomes clear that Huai-jang was referring to the routine practice of sitting cross-legged, for he said that dhyāna does not consist in sitting down or any other posture, and that the Buddha-mind has no abiding-place. This conversation bore fruit, as Ma-tsu (*q.v.*) became the originator of the koan method later on.

Broken Tile Koan. See under Kyogen.

Buddha. A man of royal family who lived in northern India, probably from about 560 to 480 B.C. As a young man, though having no troubles of his own, he became so deeply impressed with the sufferings of human beings that he decided to go around to all the yogis and teachers he could find to see if they could tell him the cause and cure of human misery. It was notable that he felt that there just *must* be a solution to this problem. However, none could satisfy him, but at last, while sitting in meditation under a peepul tree (henceforth called the bodhi-tree or bo-tree), he experienced complete illumination and understanding, and discovered the way of life for the cessation of suffering, which was based on goodness and harmlessness and was entirely in conformity with human experience and reason, although it also transcended it.

After illumination Buddha walked up and down the Ganges valley for forty-nine years, giving his knowledge freely to all.

Buddha taught that the goal which he had reached was within the scope of every man who would determine to have a pure heart with only love for all beings and no hatred at all, and with a mind so dedicated to truth, eliminating all wishful thinking or leaning on ceremonies or on other people, that it reached the borders of illumination, and then through meditation surrendered itself to the reception of the higher light, the reality beyond bodily or mental processes.

Zenists speak of the state of illumination – which must not even be called a state as that is a mental conception – as the Buddha-mind, or the true self-nature, which will replace the mistaken self-image which the human mind has built up from day to day in each person by its erroneous self-explanations, and its foolish cravings and self-pride.

Buddha nature. The same as self-nature (*q.v.*).

Buddhi. The faculty sometimes called understanding, by which a thing is known in its wholeness, not by some part or quality of it. All mental comparisons of the thing with other things are therefore considered to taint this knowledge. A familiar example is that of a piece of rope lying on the path. In this little story a villager comes along in the dusk of evening and gives a jump because he mistakes it for a snake. However, fuller inspection shows it to be a piece of rope. The reference to something else, or even to oneself in relation to the rope, must be set aside, for his direct vision. Even the desire to know something about something, the mental motive, is a hindrance. The wholeness of a thing is not to be known from the parts of it, but the parts are truly known only in relation to the whole. When a student has assembled all the data on a given matter, and when he sees them all together – in their mutually indispensable relationship – or, in brief, when the data becomes for him integral, then he *understands* or really knows. The fact is that *meanings* derive from wholes, not from parts. When a student *understands* something which previously he was only trying to understand, there comes knowledge which is not thought. When knowledge comes and is recognized as such, thought ceases. Knowing and thinking are not at all the same. The 'click' of knowing is more akin to perception than to thought.

Some will assert, no doubt correctly, that this direct knowledge does not cancel out ordinary knowledge, but supplements it. Just as the development of mentality in ordinary affairs does not preclude but actually assists bodily action, so the pure vision of the full awareness can actually help the mind in its work of knowing and the body in its accurate acting with reference to its environment.

The buddhic moment has also been compared rightly or wrongly to what is known as an experience of rapture, brought on perhaps by some grand piece of natural scenery. There is an exclamation, 'Oh, wonderful, wonderful!' Afterwards the person says, perhaps, 'I never knew what beauty was till now.' In the moment of rapture, even 'I' was forgotten, though not absent, but now, in the review or the description or even the comment, the relating of it to I or to anything else destroys the vision, even though a radiance from it permanently remains. The buddhi must be considered also as feeling as well as knowing. In seeing another person in a buddhic way, there would be the same perfect vision, or perfect empathy.

Buddhism and Zen. Zen looks back to Buddha as its founder and authority. Its place in the field of Buddhism is shown by its position in the course of history of that religion. From the beginning Buddha's doctrine excluded theism and an ultimate heaven. As theism involves a prime mover, even if impersonal, Buddha rejected it on the ground that the very conception of a mover stands in the way of the realization of the truth about man and the world, because it implies a mental category. Any sort of thinkable heaven as a permanent place or state, objective or subjective, was also rejected by him on the same grounds.

All this, however, did not militate against the discovery of the essential truth or the nature of fundamental reality, which Buddha claimed to have realized, and to be able to show others the way to realize. To this end he walked up and down the Ganges valley for over forty years, preaching his doctrine and the application of it to life.

This was not a negative proposition. If the known things of the world and the known thoughts of the mind were rejected, it was not because of absence of knowledge, but because of a better knowledge. If reason was rejected in this search and discovery, it was because something better than reason had been found – and yet the discovery was not contrary to reason nor contrary to the ethical life.

Zen followed Buddha in adhering to these propositions. It differed from some of the acceptances in that it proposed as its aim a new seeing by the individual. It therefore proposed as its way of life an attitude called meditative (zenic) – meditative in all the business of life, not merely sitting and withdrawing for a while to attend to the contents of the mind and to the working of the mind in the absence of new sense-impacts.

Immediately after Buddha's death a Council of about 500 monks sat for more than six months, and made a collection of Buddha's discourses, and put them in two groups – teachings and rules of conduct. These became called the Theravāda – the doctrine according to the elders. Two more councils (one about 100 years later and another about 150 years still later) added more to the collection and condemned wrong ideas and practices. This Theravāda became standard practice in the south of India, and so exists to this day in Ceylon, Burma, Thailand and Indonesia.

All along, however, there were discontented groups who considered the orthodox teaching according to the elders insufficiently inclusive, and these developed mostly in the north of India, and, at last, led to the great Council of Kashmir, held about A.D. 70, called the Fourth Council, but ignored or rejected by the southern schools. It was from this fourth council that what later came to be called the Mahāyāna (the Great Way) form of Buddhism received its major impetus. This movement attained great eminence when a book was written by Ashwaghosha about A.D. 100, entitled in English *The Awakening of Faith in the Mahāyāna*. Two of its chief doctrines were that of the ālaya consciousness (*q.v.*) and the 'suchness' or 'thusness' (tathatā, *q.v.*).

It was from this school of thought that Zen arose, with its doctrine of the universality of the Buddha-nature – therefore the possible attainment by 'direct transmission' without expressibility in words and therefore beyond verbal teachings, which, however useful in their limited field, could not lead to the discovery of the true 'home' (ālaya) consciousness, which is 'void' (shūya) of all comparison with the things and thoughts of the sensuous or the mental world – not '*a* void', of course, in any scientific or philosophic sense.

Bushido. The moral code of the Samurai (military class), as related to the Zen discipline. It happened that Zen came to Japan early in the Kamakura period, when the Samurai had just established a dictatorship. The arts and skills of Zen, as applied to swordsmanship, archery, etc. (see under Arts of Zen) strongly appealed to these people.

C

Ch'an. Chinese modification of the Sanskrit word *dhyāna*, which means meditation. The word was further altered to Zen when the teaching reached Japan. It was also known as hsin tsung, mind doctrine, which did not here mean the common mind as usually understood, but the ultimate mind, the Buddha-mind.

Meditation is defined by Patanjali, the author of the *Yoga Sūtras*, as a continuous flow of thought upon a subject of concentration, but is not so regarded by the Zenists. With them it is rather the prolonged or persistent effort in consciousness to become directly aware of those sources of consciousness in us which make us strive to live and to 'more live'. This is not mere thinking, because thinking is always directly or indirectly related to the environment and the senses, even when it is so-called abstract thinking.

At first Chanists were isolated men whose idea was to lead a life in harmony with everything in Nature, and to meditate for the attainment of peace or tranquillity and the opening up of intuition. They had no temples, but some of them had groups of followers or disciples. In course of time monasteries of various sects, coming to respect these men very highly, began to appoint them as Heads of their foundations. Later on came Ch'an monasteries and temples, with their own Heads. Still, even now there are (or perhaps were until very recently) many isolated and independent Ch'an Masters. It was always a feature of the Ch'an life to do a fair share of manual work. On the other hand most of the early Chanists did not give much attention to Buddhist literature, which began to provide much material descriptive of meditation and its results for them only after the arrival from India of Kumārajīva (*q.v.*), Bodhidharma (*q.v.*) and others.

The cult of Ch'an reached its height in the T'ang and Sung periods, mostly among the less educated strata of society. After Hui-neng (*q.v.*) there were five definite Schools of Ch'an started by his disciples.

The following noted Chinese Zen Masters and teachers of old times are itemized in this dictionary:

Chao-chou, Chih-i, Ching-tu, Fa-jung or Ho-yun, Fa-tsang, Fa-yen, Hsing Szu, Hsuan-chien, Hsuan-tsang, Huao-jang, Hua-yen, Huang-po, Hui-ke, Hui-neng, Hui-yuan, Hung-jen, Hwei-hai or Pai-chang, Lao-tsu, Lin-chi or I'hsuan, Ma-tsu or Tao-i, Mu-chou,

Nan-ch'uan, Niao-ka, Pa-chio Hui-ch'ing, Po-yin, Seng-tsan, Shen-hui, Shen-shin, Shen-shiu, Shih-tou, Tao-an, Tao-hsin, Tao-hsuan, Tao-sheng, Tsao-shan, Tung-shan, Tuo-yuan, Yun-men.

Chao-Chou (778–897). In Japanese, Joshu or Jushin. Zen Master of the early Chang Dynasty, noted for his acuteness and profundity. He was author of the koan: 'If all things are to be returned to the One, to where is that One to be returned?' He objected very much to what he called verbalism, or mere use of words without penetration. He lived to the age of nearly 120.

Chih-i (531–597). Also known as Chigi (in Japanese), or K'e Fu, or by his full name Chich-che Tai-shih. A founder of the Tien-Tai (Tendai) School of Buddhism. A two-sided philosopher, who gave part time to intellectual studies, and part time to the practice of samādhi. In course of time, however, his followers leaned more towards intellection, and became quite opposed to Zen. Chih-i was the founder of thirty-five monasteries. He also obtained enough contributions to make fifteen complete collections of the Buddhist scriptures, and wrote a book on philosophy and meditation which is still widely read today.

Chih-i was a great scholar, and the excellence, and even elegance, of Paramārtha's translation into Chinese of the *Shraddhotpāda Shāstra* (*Awakening of Faith*) is considered to be largely due to his assistance in that work. It was to Chih-i (K'e Fu) that Lin-chi explained his fourfold system. (See under Lin-chi.)

Children. Can a child get Satori or illumination? There are different opinions, but most Zenists and certainly those in the monasteries of Japan believe that the mind has to be developed first, and then the mature mind can be guided into the right way by koans, etc. Still, one must allow for occasional precocious cases; but one supposes that a non-intelligent child could not. The story of John the Baptist – that he received the Holy Ghost while still in his mother's womb – may have some bearing on this.

China, Buddhist Sects in. Ten schools of Buddhism came to be developed in China. They were:

Therevāda (Hīnayāna) Schools	Abhidharmakosha Satyasiddhi Vinaya	These did not last long.
Mahāyāna Schools	Mādhyamika	Elaborated and completed by Chi-sang (549–623).
	Yogāchāra	Developed by Hsuan-tsang and his pupil Kuei-chi (632–82).
	Meditation (chan)	(See under Bodhidharma, Hui-neng, etc.).
	Mystical	Developed by Subhakārasinha.

26

Chinese Schools	{ Hua-yen Tien-tai Pure Land

China, Zen in. Zen is regarded as having become the special Buddhism of China because it suited the Chinese mind, which always concerned itself with things as they are rather than with speculation as to how they may be different from what they seem, or may be made different from what they are. It is not considered in zenic meditation that the practice will bring to light *something about* the object which was not seen before, but that in the contact with the whole object there will be a direct revelation. It is akin, may we say, to the experience of the senses, in which red is red and green is green, except that the focus of attention is turned from an object to the subject, and so one's 'self-nature' in these circumstances is faced and revealed. Just as red is red, so self is self, and just as the red is tainted if mixed up with other colours so is the self-nature lost sight of when spoiled by passion and desire.

Buddha was great enough to realize both the 'Indian' outlook with its creative logic (both speculative and practical), and the 'Chinese' outlook with its directness and immediateness. Thus he could over-come or transcend racial bias which, while favouring certain growths of man keeps other growths in obscurity for the time being (just as a child in the mathematics period in school is not aware of historical studies). An instance of this came out when Buddha asked the monks to step on the ground and tell him what they felt. The monks de-scribed the earth, the gravel, etc., and were surprised when Buddha exclaimed: 'What! Did you not feel the foot?' Carrying the system further we realize that in all experience we should be able to realize our essential 'self-nature', not as an object among objects, nor as a subject among objects, but just as it is. As red is red and reveals itself as such, with no comparison with anything else, so I am I in my own self-nature. This incident of the foot can be placed alongside the in-cident of the flower which gave Mahākāshyapa his revelation. (See under Zen.)

Ching-tu. In Japanese, Jodo. The Pure Land Sect (*q.v.*).

Circles. Various kinds of circles drawn in the air or on the ground be-came frequent in the Ikyo schools, to indicate the contents of en-lightenment. One teacher was credited with teaching by means of nearly a hundred of them. Kyozan in particular used and developed them.

A set of seven circles or discs came to be used, especially in the Soto School, as a sort of cosmological dialectic. Of these seven, five repre-sented the 'five ranks' within the field of relative existence, and so were regarded as helpful to know on the way to enlightenment. The

27

first two were a black disc and a white one – ● and ○. The first, sometimes called darkness, represented the Absolute, also the Void. The second is therefore the relative, a principle which is always present wherever anything at all is. It is therefore not properly a circle as drawn, but a white disc. The circle gives the idea of a circumscribed field because of its peripheral line, but the field of relativity is not a circumscribed area in any sense. It is rather what the Hindus call space (ākāsha) which is not room (avakāsha). If one were to cut out a paper circle and hold it up and look at it one could see its circularity by its edge, that is, where it leaves off, not by a line, where it is stopped. It is therefore sometimes called 'brightness' – or, shall we say, manifestness?

From these two we proceed to the five ranks, the signs for which are ◕, ◔, ◑, ○ and ◕. These represent the five stages of the disciple's way, as indicated in Sozan Honkaju's 'Lord and Vassal' simile. In 1 he finds that the lord is looking down upon the servant; in 2 he identifies himself as the devoted and willing servant; in 3 he realizes himself as merely peripheral to the lord; in 4 he realizes that he is within the lord, and in 5 the servant has become all lord and they are one, or in complete unity.

Every disciple was to realize these steps in his own life, as they successively arose, that is, they could not be mentalized and looked forward to, because it could not be known what they are until they are experienced and then recognized. Because, however, the use of these symbols tended to the intrusion of mentalizing, Dogen Kigen, who was the founder of Japanese Soto, rejected them.

In connection with the enlightenment in the last of these five stages one may be reminded of a parallel to this among the Sufis. The story goes that a disciple wanted to know what became of a man when he reached 'unification' and became 'one with God'. He asked, 'Does the man still go on?' 'Did I not say,' replied the Teacher, 'that God goes on?' God was always one with the man, but now the man is one with God – the Lord or the Absolute. Yet any anticipatory thought of that union destroys it by its necessary erroneousness.

Compassion. This was so much stressed by Buddha that many regard it as a prerequisite for enlightenment, as, in fact, opening the doors of the mind to the world of *life* around us – just as important as the senses are for knowing the material world around us. From this comes the Bodhisattwa vow. It is within the Zen programme, because the Zenist shuts no doors, but finds the Buddha-nature in everything.

Yet the compassion must be genuine. 'Why did I take the trouble to catch the cockroach in the bathroom, and put it gently out of doors?' Was it self-righteousness, or was it the genuine compassion which is fellow-feeling?

Concepts. When in Zen there is the advice to give up all concepts, it must of course include the concept of no-concept. The difficulty or paradox of this is solved by an understanding of what samādhi (*q.v.*) is.

Consciousness. It is of two kinds. There is (1) the consciousness of something, called sanjnā or vijnā in Sanskrit, and (2) the being of consciousness itself, knowing itself as such, without any object (or mirror), named prajnā in Sanskrit. Number (2) is sometimes called 'pure consciousness' – that consciousness which we have, or rather are, even when we have not noticed it.

Cow-herding Simile, The. This is given in a series of ten pictures representing the cow-herder (Zenist or meditator) as (1) looking for the bull, (2) finding the footprints of it, (3) perceiving it, (4) catching it, (5) herding or taming it, (6) riding the bull home, (7) back home resting, the bull forgotten, (8) both self and bull forgotten or transcended, (9) the man now in his own true nature or abode, and (10) the man back in the world 'with bliss-bestowing hands'. The ten pictures are nicely presented by a modern Japanese woodblock artist, Tomi Kichiro Tokoriki in *Zen Flesh, Zen Bones*, compiled by Paul Reps from transcriptions by Nyogen Senzaki. The original pictures were drawn by Kakuan, of the Rinzai school, in the twelfth century.

There is an older set of pictures, from the Zen teacher Seikyo, which represented the change of the cow from black to white. These showed first the man chasing the cow, which is all black, then the man catching the cow which is wildly struggling and still all black; then we have the cow, now with the head white, following the man; next he is tying it to a tree and the neck also is white; after that we see it following him without a lead and with the trunk of its body white; then lying peacefully with all but its tail and buttocks white while the man sits playing his flute; next the man is meditating while the all-white cow quietly drinks water from a stream; then both appear in the sky. Next to the last picture shows the man again in the world, without any cow, and finally there is only an empty circle. A modern set of these consists of ten pictures, but it is said that in the original Seikyo set there were only six.

Creation. Zen does not concern itself with cosmogony, or creation and dissolution. All the same, there is a view of creation as separation, not as production, which is very much in harmony with Zen. When there is creation there is addition, there are two things where there was one before. But it can equally be said, you have only split one thing into two, and separated them. When God at first made man, he had a glass of blessings standing by. 'This be thy portion, child . . .' This thought, from one of Emerson's poems, applies to all things. Fundamentally, all are one, and none can escape the unity. So, in Zen, it is not considered that self-nature can be realized by a process of separation or denial.

This agrees with the doctrine of creation as māyā, which is common in India. The first step in māyā is 'veiling' (āvarana). By that the one becomes dual, in such a manner that there is temporary entity of what we may call the separate parts – the observer or subject is a subjective entity; the observed or object is an objective entity. This is the first *mental* act in a baby's life – the ascription of its feelings (of pain or pleasure) to an object which is regarded as 'an object' or entity. Such, for example, would be the mother's breast; first it gives rise to pleasure; only afterwards it becomes *known* as something which gives pleasure. Special attention is then given to that; unpleasing things are either ignored or avoided. So arises ignorance or limited knowledge. Something is attended to; some other things are left out. This is the form of knowing called avidyā (ignorance or error). It is a veiling of part of the reality. The 'me' arises similarly with reference to the body and mind, which nevertheless we are logical enough to call 'mine'.

The second part of the 'creation' process is called 'vikshepa' (literally, projection). It is action. A *limited* idea is now impressed on the environment by means of an action. This is the creation proper, or it may be destruction, of course. Now there stands before the man the clock, or the wheelbarrow, let us say, which he has made. But it represents a limited idea, and so is called a māyā. It veils, not reveals the truth of life.

This doctrine was accepted by Buddha, but not adopted by the Zenists, who if consistent and thorough-going, do not want to pursue any form of science or philosophy in their meditations. They consider that many doctrines of Buddha which are quite true were intended for the 'weaker brethren' who are not ready for essential meditation. It is arguable that Buddha used the title arhat (*q.v.*), which means ready, for those who were capable of the zenic endeavour.

D

Dai-funshin. Great perseverance. One of the three essentials of Zen practice.

Dai-gidan. Great doubt. One of the three essentials of Zen practice. It is in connection with this that it has been said that at first mountains are (or seem to be) mountains, then they are not mountains, and finally they are mountains again.

Daijozen. Mahāyāna Zen. Meditation for the purpose of seeing into one's own nature and realizing the Way, i.e. kensho-godo, leading to satori directly.

Dai-shinkon. Great faith. One of the three essentials of Zen practice. The proposition of Zen that all have the Buddha-nature is required, so that the aspirant may proceed with confidence. On looking round, the student seeing such a variety of beings acquires dai-gidan, great doubt. Still, as the statement has come from Zen Masters, he is inspired with great determination, dai-funshin, and perseverance to find the truth for himself. (See under Faith.)

Daitokuji. A famous Rinzai monastery of Kyoto, former capital of Japan.

Daruma. Japanese name for Bodhidharma (*q.v.*).

Death. As regards mundane affairs, most Zenists share in the usual Buddhist beliefs. In this case the belief is that though the body dies, the skandhas live on, and are reborn, subject to constant modification. Zenists rarely write or think about this, however, as they are intent on realization of the Buddha-mind here and now. They are also intent on the cessation of attachment, not on the building of better or greater future lives, in this world or any other. Still, without this belief they would not see how persons will some time realize Nirvāna, even though they may not proceed to do so until after many lifetimes.

Debts, The Four. To parents, for life; to other living beings, for help; to the government, for peace; and to Buddha, for enlightenment. It is with these in view that some aspirants take the Bodhisattwa vow, or else resolve to help others when they obtain enlightenment. (See also under Karma.)

Dengyo Daishi. Japanese scholar who returned from a visit to China, and brought back the Tendai school of thought in A.D. 804.

Dhāranīs. Sayings which people of various sects repeat on certain regular occasions or in times of stress to sustain or hold up their ardour or their faith. Such is the Zen 'Gate, gate, etc.' (*q.v.*). Other sects have their own special dhāranīs, such as the 'Namo Omito Fu' of the Pure Land Sect, or the 'Namo myoho renge kyo' of the Nichirenists.

Dharma, or Dhamma. In Ch'an and Zen philosophy it means self-nature, which is a void, as far as anything known by mind, or thinkable, is concerned. It is to be noted, of course, that on account of this proviso the void must not be thought of as what the *mind* calls a void, or empty space. The combination of void and self-nature can be explained by stating that the essential nature of man is not of the nature of body or of mind or of anything known by them. It contains the assertion, however, that there *is* this essential self-nature in man – indeed, in every living being.

The use of the word dharma for this means that this self-nature is the support or basis of everything else, including body and mind. The word dharma comes from a root which means to support or sustain.

The word dharma is used also to refer to the teachings of Buddha. In this case it is often translated 'The Law'. In Sanskrit writings in general it has come to mean the social law, and by further extension 'duty', as, for example, in the sentence, 'By doing his own duty (dharma) a man reaches perfection; the duty of another is full of danger,' which is sometimes broadly interpreted as 'By acting according to his own nature – talents and abilities', and sometimes narrowly, as 'By obeying the rules of the caste into which he was born'. Either of these interpretations will agree with the technical term *sahaja*, which literally means 'born with'.

Dharma-dhātu. The Law doctrine (see under Avatanshaka Sūtra and Gānda-vyūha). This Law is, however, not one of mere material causation, but is the reality beyond both being and non-being. Its causality is interpenetrative and over-all, not merely successive. Perhaps its nature may be crudely represented by saying that just as day does not cause night nor night day (although they invariably succeed one another), so the ultimate causality is utterly inclusive and not successive, so that the convergence of all things is the cause of each, and each is effective in the causation of all the others. In this manner the Law holds everything in its hand, just as the rotation of the earth holds both night and day.

Dharmakāya. The essential nature or 'essence-body' of a buddha. (See under Kāyas.)

Diamond Sūtra, The. In Sanskrit, Vajrachchhedika, which is a portion of the Prajnā-Pāramitā Sūtra. A Buddhist scripture in the Sanskrit language much used for meditation by followers and successors of the Fifth and Sixth Patriarchs.

In an assembly of monks (bhikkus) numbering 1250 the venerable Subhuti got up and asked the Buddha how they should proceed to attain the perfect wisdom (anuttara-samyak-sambuddhi). He then explained at considerable length six practices (pāramitās) – of charity (dāna), of unselfishness (shīla), of patience (kshānti), of resolution (vīrya), of meditation (dhyāna), and of direct knowledge or wisdom (prajnā). Each of these in turn was related to the freedom from separate selfhood involved in their respective perfection since the true selfness or suchness (tathatā) of all beings and things is a void (shūnya) as far as separate characteristics are concerned. In the detailed explanations of these essential matters in the Diamond Sūtra there is very much food for zenic meditation. Finally, Subhuti asked by what name this scripture should be known, and Buddha said as the Vajrachchedika Prajnā Pāramitā. Vajra means a diamond, because it is impregnable.

Discipline, The Triple. Shīla, dhyāna and prajnā. Shīla is good conduct or virtue; dhyāna is meditation, and prajnā is wisdom. Hui-neng has the following verse on this topic:

To free the mind from all impurity is the Shīla of the Essence of Mind.
To free the mind from all disturbance is the Dhyāna of the Essence of Mind.
That which neither increases nor decreases is the vajra (diamond).
Diamond is here used as a symbol of Essence of Mind.

Dogen. One of the greatest figures in the history of Zen. Born in Japan in 1200, he lived 53 years. He first studied Zen under Esai in Japan; afterwards, when 24 years old, went to China and became proficient in the za-zen (q.v.) method current in the Ts'ao Tung (Soto) school there, and finally returned after four years to Japan and founded the Soto (q.v.) school, which became the largest Zen sect of Buddhism in Japan, and now has about 15,000 temples there with about 7,000,000 members. Dogen wrote his teaching down for the guidance of this sect, his best known work being the Shobogenzo, which means *The Eye of the True Law*.

His attitude may be understood from the following extract. 'The burning of incense, the bowing before the Buddha's image and prayer to him, confession of sin and the reading of the Sūtras are all, from the very beginning of one's discipleship, wholly unnecessary. The one and only thing required is to free oneself from the bondage of mind and body alike, putting the Buddha's own seal upon yourself. If you do this as you sit in ecstatic meditation the whole universe itself turns into enlightenment. This is what I mean by the Buddha's seal.' This comes out even more strongly in another part of the Shobogenzo:

'What good are such actions as reading the sūtras and saying the nembutsu? How futile to think that merits accrue from merely moving the tongue and raising the voice. If you think this covers Buddhism you are far from the truth. Constant repetition of the nembutsu is worthless, like a frog in a spring field croaking night and day.'

It was Dogen who connected Zen with the politics or national life of Japan, on account of his advocacy of the 'restoration of power to the Throne'.

Doshin. In Chinese, Tao-hsin. Fourth Chinese Zen Patriarch.

...isai (1141–1215). A Japanese monk who introduced the original Lin-chi school of Zen into Japan in 1191, and established monasteries at Kyoto and Kamakura with the aid of the Emperor. He also brought the tea ceremony to Japan, though since then it has been somewhat changed.

...ka or Yeka. Hui-ke (*q.v.*).

...kai. Noted for his comments on 48 important koans.

...nlightenment. See Satori.

...no or Yeno. Hui-neng (*q.v.*).

...quanimity. Samachittatā. No matter what comes, the man who has equanimity is not troubled in mind. This is due to his realization of the Buddha-mind, his own true nature, of which he is conscious along with all the other things. A feeble mental reflection of this is seen in the idea that the human soul can outride any storm, also the well-known statement of the Hindu scriptures that all comes equally to the sage; clay is as good as gold. This is also vajra – the hardness of the diamond and the power of the thunderbolt. It was once asked if this is only for sages and not for ordinary people, the answer was that when the ordinary man has realized this through meditation (Zen) he is a sage. The sage does not need to be a mental genius, any more than he needs to be an athlete.

...thics and Beliefs. Does Zen cancel or replace the general rules of con-duct and the common beliefs (such as reincarnation and karma) taught by Buddha? The answer is that the average Buddhist Zenist does not alter these when he takes up Zen. He still thinks that if he does not gain realization of Buddha-mind during the lifetime of the present body (anyhow, it may be cut off by war, famine, pestilence or accident at any time) he will be born again somewhere else in an-other body and continue his quest. And even though he holds, as practically all Buddhists do, to the non-continuity of himself as a self such as he recognizes and now identifies himself to be, he believes in Buddha's doctrine of the continuity of the bundle of skandhas (*q.v.*).

35

As long as that bundle is held together by the thought of self it will continue; from time to time there will always be body, feelings, perception, tendencies or habits, and mentality, though continuously modified, as long as the error of 'selfhood' lasts. It is something like the case of the old one-hoss shay. One year it had new shafts, another new wheels, another new boards, and so on until it was all changed, and yet it was 'the same old one-hoss shay'.

With the coming of Zenic realization, however, something suddenly occurs; now we may change our simile from the story of the one-hoss shay to that of the grub and the butterfly. Ask the butterfly: does it think it was ever a grub? Ask even the man who believes in reincarnation and also in evolution whether he believes he was ever a monkey – and he will, if a thinker, probably say: 'No, not "I"; but sometime there was a sudden descent as it were from the infinite of the human mind principle (something not in the monkey), and then the "I" which is what I am was suddenly born from the infinite. And so it will be with another borning when it comes, when this present "I" in the perfection of its worship surrenders itself once and for all to that which has all along been tickling it (as it were) from above or within, or rather from the unknown. There will then be a "new birth", not the same as a "rebirth".'

Other similes are that of the child and the man or woman, and the leg and the arm. The child cannot think of what it means to be a man or woman. If he tries to think of it he will only catch on to externals, not to the state of mind. Yet he knows that something will come when the time is ripe. Meantime he is developing capacities and, we hope, health and strength. The leg serves the arm and gains from what the arm then does. Briefly, evolution proceeds by steps as in a staircase, not as an inclined plane or ramp.

F

Faith. It has been said that faith implies a division and thus a duality, and so is contrary to Zen. Against this we may put the well-known statement that Zen requires great faith, great questioning and great perseverance. The fact is, of course, that Zen faith is not faith in the sense of worshipping or relying upon some other being, but faith in the existence of the Buddha-mind and in meditation as the means to its realization. And even then it is not that *you* realize it, but that it is realized or fulfilled in you. Just as body cannot comprehend mind, so also mind cannot comprehend Buddha-mind, and just as when mind develops in an animal – let us say – it does not destroy the animal body, so when the Buddha-mind appears it does not destroy the ordinary mind.

Faith, then, is the 'thin end of the wedge' of Buddha-mind, always present in some degree, but not usually enough to dislodge the self-image or personality picture made by the ordinary mind. It is probably that which causes what the Western theologians call our 'divine discontent', whereby the best that we can think of is still unsatisfying. And it must have been some similar recognition which caused Emerson to affirm (rather unexpectedly to some) that 'Worship is the flowering and completion of human culture.'

Fa-jung. Also called Ho-yun. An independent teacher in the time of the Fourth Patriarch, who lived on Mount Niu-t'ou. He leaned towards the old orthodox Zen, and started the Niu-t'ou or Gozusan School, which did not long survive its founder.

Fa-tsang. Founder of the Hua-yen (Kegon) School. He enumerated six contemplations necessary for understanding the Avatanshaka scripture, viz., on the serenity of the fundamental Mind; on the source of all things as Mind; on the wonderful interrelatedness of all things; on the true being or suchness (tathatā) of all; on the way in which all things can appear in mind without mutual exclusion; and on how any one thing is an indicator of all things.

Fa-Yen Zen Sect. Hogen Zen. Founded by Wen I of Ch'ing Liang. Generally known by his posthumous title of Fa Yen. It has died away. The teaching of this school was that all things are hsin, a term which included both mind and heart. This means that every form in the world has been produced by mind, and therefore not only represents it, but presents it. (See also Hogen.)

Fear. There are several reasons why the Zenist has little or no fear. He is not looking to something or someone else for his protection or his salvation; he is confident that he has in himself the seed of perfection, and he, if a Buddhist, believes that he will not be cut off from opportunity because as long as he needs it the law of Karma will place it before him. Just as he has confidence in himself, he has confidence in the cosmos – that it is not chaos, and, in modern terms, the river cannot rise above its source, that is, the ethic and spirituality of man are not accidental, but express the fact that he now touches the ethical and spiritual truths or laws of Nature, just as with the coming of mind there was the discovery of law and order in Nature.

Modern psychology may also be applied to this. The well-known James–Lange theory indicates that we fear first and know that we fear afterwards. This built-in fear is a painful feeling in the budding animal mind whereby something harmful in the past indicates its presence, and this instinct or unconscious or subconscious memory starts off the alertness which is so necessary in animal life. Man hears a sound or feels something which produces fear in him. Only after that he realizes 'I have fear'. And after that he uses, or ought to use, his intelligence. But, strictly, fear is rarely useful in civilized human life. Caution should take its place.

Finger Pointing at the Moon. A warning by Buddha not to mistake the teaching or the teacher (the pointing finger) for the moon (the goal). In modern terms, if you follow a Zen or other Master take care to know and follow the masterness of the master, not merely the outer form or kāya (q.v.). There is also a classic entitled *Finger Pointing at the Moon*, which contains many stories of the sayings of Zen Masters. (See under Sayings.)

Foot and Ground. See under Nature, the Teacher.

G

Gānda-vyūha. A portion (about a quarter) of the Avatanshaka Sūtra much used in the Hua-yen school (*q.v.*), which promotes the 'Law doctrine' (Dharma-dhātu) greatly valued in the Hua-yen school. The background story of the sūtra is an account of how a young pilgrim seeking enlightenment visited about fifty teachers.

'Gate, Gate'. The first words of a mantra uttered by the Bodhisattwa Avalokiteshwara, when he came to the end of his severe mental struggles and broke the last ties of 'self', or relative identity. The whole mantra runs: 'Gate, gate, paragate, parasangate, bodhi, swāhā,' and is translated in Goddard's *Buddhist Bible* as follows: 'Gone, gone, gone to the other shore; safely passed to that other shore, O Prajnāpāramitā! So mote it be!' The last word (swāhā) is used at the end of many mantras of old India. It is explained in the Gopālatāpani Upanishad that swāhā means the 'power by which the world goes on evolving', so no doubt the translator felt that 'So mote it be' would be taken as an affirmative assertion expressing assent, and union in the use of that power. It thus is understood to give powerful effect to the mantra, not mere acquiescence to it. The te in 'gate' is pronounced 'tay'.

Avalokiteshwara's mantra occurs at the end of the Mahaprajnā-Pāramitā-Hridaya Sūtra. Hridaya means the heart, or essence of the Sūtra. This Sūtra or Scripture is short (only a few pages) and constitutes a very terse summing-up of the meaning of Prajnā and enlightenment.

Gāthās. Verses of four lines, such as that given by the Sixth Patriarch in response to the test proposed by the Fifth Patriarch. (See under Hui-neng.) The following examples of classical gāthās are from *The Transmission of the Lamp*, translated by Lu K'uan Yu.

> The mind-ground holds the seeds
> Which sprout when falls the all-pervading rain.
> The wisdom-flower of instantaneous awakening
> Cannot fail to bear the bodhi fruit.

This was chanted by Hui-neng when transmitting the Dharma to his disciples. Another gāthā, both beautiful and significant, and very Zenic, reads:

> The bamboo shadows are sweeping the stairs,
> But no dust is stirred;
> Moonlight penetrates into the depth of the pool,
> But no trace is left in the water.

An example from India, given by the twenty-sixth Patriarch to his successor, runs:

> The true nature (of the Self) lies in the ground of Mind.
> It has neither head nor tail.
> It manifests to meet the needs of living beings.
> For want of better words we call it wisdom.

A collection of many gāthās constitutes one of the twelve divisions of the Mahāyāna canon.

Gedo Zen. Zen or meditation practices outside the Buddhist framework, such as Christian mysticism, Hindu Raja Yoga, and the 'quiet sitting' of Confucius. As an extension of Bombo Zen, Gedo Zen has been mentioned in connection with such items as charming sparrows by a sort of hypnotism and walking unharmed on swords. It is included within the term Mushinjo.

Genjo. Hsuan Tsang (*q.v.*).

Gijo. One of the three antecedent requisites for the attainment of satori. A state of doubt or mental tension. The others are great faith and great perseverance.

Go-i. A set of five rungs in a Zen course or ladder of meditation, having to do with pairs of opposites of a very inclusive kind, such as the absolute and the relative, emptiness and form, li (the universal) and shih (the particular). Having selected a pair (called sho and hen) the student proceeds to view the hen in the sho (*e.g.*, the many in the One). In the second step he views the sho in the hen (the One in the many, for if there are many each must be a one, and if there is One it must include the many). Thirdly, he views 'the coming from the sho' (how the hen comes from the sho, how the many derives from the One). Next comes shi (arriving), and last (and fifth) ken (both) chi (in) to (established).

The student who can follow these five steps with regard to many pairs of opposites of the kind which refer to general and particular or inclusion and exclusion will have gone far on this way. The subject is too complex and extensive to detail here. Dr D. T. Suzuki has given us a full description of it in *Zen Buddhism and Psychoanalysis*.

Good and Evil. In the three essential requirements for Zen we do not find a classification or judgement of things according to 'good' and 'bad'. This is not the discriminatory process for Zen, but rather the discrimination of what is and what is not, or in a word 'truth'. It implies, however, a release from the bondage of affective bias, so is in agreement with the principle of compensation in life as expounded in Emerson's essay on Compensation.

It would not be zenic to say, however, that we appreciate the good as a contrast from the bad. A man who had had asthma once remarked to a friend, 'You do not appreciate the pleasure of breathing easily, because you have never been deprived of it.' No doubt the experience of the pain directed the man's attention to the appreciation of the pleasure, but he should have done it positively by direct perception, and not been directed to it the hard way, by the pointing finger of pain. Otherwise, one would be compelled to the paradox that only those who have been murdered are in a position to appreciate life. In Zen the three requirements are great faith, great doubt and great determination – these are the 'goods', and they are something that we *are*, not something that we *have*. There is no objection, probably, to our relating of these three 'goods' to the indubitable facts that we *feel*, we *think* and we *will*.

Goodness, Truth and Beauty. It has been asked whether these are of any interest to Zenists. It is definite that Zen does not aim at enlightenment by 'getting away from all this'. On the contrary, most of them agree to the statement: 'All objects, even the inanimate, expound the Dharma.' This does not mean, however, that they would approve of aiming at Nirvāna through seeing or creating Goodness, Truth or Beauty. On the contrary, they prefer naturalness, and the tathatā or thing-in-itself of every object or being (bhūta).

Naturalness is concerned with health as resulting from factual acceptance of organic development. In modern thought we know that the body has come to be as it is as the result of the preservation of favourable adaptations in the course of heredity, and that sins against this are the bodily sins, whether in action or in thought. The three ideals herein mentioned appear to be concerned in a similar manner with the *relations* between the organism and its environment, with which the *mind* has everything to do. They are the criteria of mental health, in the business of feeling, thinking and action. This being the case, meditation in India has been very much concerned with them. Not so Zen meditation, however, which aims at the Dharma, the support and basis. The very word Dharma comes from a Sanskrit root meaning 'to support,' and in reference to the three departments of modern scientific study – matter, energy and law – Zen could well say that it is Law that supports

41

the other two. Remove the law of causality, for example, and all collapses.

And yet, inasmuch as it is desirable to have health, so it is necessary in practical life where the mind operates to have mind-health which is in the three perfections – Goodness, Truth and Beauty. If these are Pāramitās, their culmination is the Prajnā, and above all the great Prajnā which reveals the Buddha-mind, and allows the aspirant to realize Enlightenment and Nirvāna.

Gunin. Hung-jen (*q.v.*).

Gyoshi. See under Soto.

H

Haiku, The. A special form of Japanese poetry in three lines, the first having five syllables, the second having seven, and the third again five. The enjoyment of this is so great in Japan that it is said there are no less than fifty magazines devoted to it.

Haiku poems are not for instruction, but are for deep enjoyment of sentiments or of knowledge. Some examples are:

> A morning glory.
>   And so, today, may seem
>   My own life story.

> The peony has fallen.
>   A few scattered petals
>   Lie on one another.

> A butterfly
>   Asleep, perched upon
>   The temple bell.

> The thief
>   Left it behind.
>   The moon at the window.

These, however, are not quite zenic, as they contain too much thought, approaching philosophy. What we may call a zenic haiku is one that causes enhanced perception, so that, as Blyth puts it, 'A haiku is not a poem; it is not literature; it is a hand beckoning, a door half-opened, a mirror wiped clean. It is a way of returning to nature ... [even] our Buddha nature.' The following are zenic examples, by Basho:

> The old pond.
>   A frog jumps in.
>   Plop.

> On a withered bough
>   A crow has stopped to perch
>   And autumn darkens.

> We gaze,
>   Even at horses,
>   This morn of snow.

It has been said that to catch the original quality or effect of such a haiku one must repeat it several times, or even many times, with deepening contact. From that comes intuition, or, better, insight. This is akin to the capacity for wonder. This faculty of wonder, or openness of mind, beyond thought, or of mind-perception (not sense-perception), is to some extent artificially induced by the form of the poem, such that it produces a poise or a series of receptive poises of thought. Suppose, instead of looking through the window and saying: 'It's raining again this morning,' one said:

> 'It is raining,
> Again,
>   This morning.'

This makes a difference, does it not? Mr R. H. Blyth has written four volumes about the haiku, full of rich information and direction, and also one volume entitled *Zen in English Literature*.

Hakuin Ekaku (1685–1768). Also called Po-yin. A Zen Master, who founded what is called the modern Rinzai School of Zen, to which the present-day Rinzai Sect Masters trace their line of transmission. His work led to the formation of the Inzan School, through Inzan Ien and the Takuju School through Takuju Kosen. He played a large part in the reviving and arranging of the teaching by koans. He was one of the very few Zen Masters who recorded their experiences in writing, which he did in his book *Orategama*. He was also the author of a poem entitled *The Song of Za-zen*.

Hekiganshu. An important Zen textbook, especially in the Rinzai Schools. It contains a collection of 100 Zen items, with poetical comments and critical annotations. (See also under Sesshin.)

Hogen Buneki. In Chinese, Fa-yen (885–958). A very learned Zen Master, who approved the method of cancellation of thought by thought, a very gentle method, the opposite of the sticks and shouts of the Rinzai School. It lent itself naturally to a missing of the point, which Hogen aimed at averting by his method of repetition. If the student said something which showed to the Master that he did not understand, the Master would not argue, but would repeat, and repeat again and again if necessary, his statement. The repetition was a rebuke, or a verbal slap, so to speak, of a very gentle kind. It was intended to make the student try again.

In the Hogen school (also called Fa-yen) the study of the Avatan-shaka Sūtra was regarded as important. Also the Kegon doctrine of the six fundamental and inseparable facts, presented in three pairs: (1 and 2) unity and multiplicity, (3 and 4) sameness and difference, (5 and 6) coming up and going out. Here was much food for meditation. On the principle of inseparateness, there must even be sameness in differences and vice-versa.

Honen. Founder of the Pure Land School in Japan (*q.v.*).

Horin-ji. Temple of the Sixth Patriarch, Hui-neng, at Sokei, not far from Canton, in the present Kwangtung Province. It was from here that Nangaku Ejo and Seigen Gyoshi spread the movement westward and southward respectively.

Hosso. After Buddhism in Japan came under Imperial protection (under the Prince Shotoku Taishi – A.D. 572–622) Hosso, founded in 635, was one of six sects which soon emerged. Of those six only the Hosso, Kegon and Ritsu now exist. The big sects of today were of later origin.

Hosso temples in Japan now number only about 40. The sect followed the Fa-hsiang idealistic school founded in China by Hsuan-tsang, the great traveller.

Hossu. A short stick, or fly-whisk. (See under sticks.)

Host and Guest. See under Soto

Ho-yu. Fa-jung (*q.v.*).

Hsin. Mind or heart. (See under Wu-nien.)

Hsing Szu. Seigen (*q.v.*).

Hoi-yun. Huang Po (*q.v.*) In Japanese, Obaku.

Hsuan-chien. Tokusan (*q.v.*).

Hsuan Tsang. Genjo, in Japanese (602–62). Famous Chinese traveller, who returned from India in 645, after a trip lasting seventeen years, in which he visited almost all the great Indian universities, both Buddhist and Hindu, also Ceylon and Persia. He brought to China several images of Buddha, and a large number of Buddhist texts, many of which he and his pupils translated. He is best known as the great historian of Indian life and thought in the seventh century.

Hsuan Tsang was an idealist, considering that all objects are produced by mind. He founded the Wei-shih (mind action) school of thought. This indicates that the world of objects is a projection of mind, and so is fourth in a series beginning with the unmanifest.

Huang Po (d. 850). Obaku, in Japanese. Founder of the Obaku Sect, and author of the *Doctrine of Universal Mind*. He was third in descent from Hui-neng, the Sixth Patriarch, and was the teacher of Rinzai. He was noted for his rough methods, in which Rinzai followed him. During his life he was also called T'uan Chi and Hsi-yun, while in Japan he is usually called Obaku.

Huang Po held the opinion that Buddha had to preach *three*

45

Vehicles of Truth, otherwise he would have done nothing at all for most of his hearers. This means there were elementary teachings for the bulk of the people (the Hinayāna), the more mystical teachings for the middle group (the Mahāyāna), but the strict Zen for those who could take it. It is to be noted that in the 'transmission without words', when Buddha held up the flower (see under Zen), only Mahākāshyapa among a large gathering of monks at that time caught the message. Still, it is to be noted also that in Buddha's description of the Noble Eightfold Path, presented in the Theravada school (or Hinayāna) the last item is 'Correct Meditation,' which gives a place for Zen in the very definite and direct description of the Way. The fact that that term, now usually translated 'meditation' was originally 'samādhi' emphasizes this point. However, it may also be argued that when Buddha prescribed this 'Correct Samādhi', he used a word, and Zen proper is the transmission without words.

Huang Po was very insistent upon 'no concepts'. This simply must refer to 'with reference to Self or True Mind', because otherwise one would be dead of starvation in a few days. One definition of 'an idiot' used to be a person who has not enough intelligence to take food placed before him, even though very hungry. Besides, Huang Po believed in karma, as when he advised his monks to have pure and passionless knowledge so as to put an end to the flow of thoughts and images, and so stop creating the karma that leads to rebirth, or at least be sure that rebirth will be as you really want it. 'Bodhisattwas,' he quotes from one of the Sūtras, 'are reborn in whatever forms they desire.' This is in accordance with the old idea in India of cessation of sankalpa, which is the making of plans for oneself, when life becomes filled with plans for others. This being so, and Huang Po's own work of teaching being in this category, there can be little doubt that the no-concept demand only means, as Buddha himself asserted, that no concepts can lead to, or apply to, the Illumination which is called 'Buddha-mind'.

Huao-jang. Nangaku Ejo (q.v.).

Hua-tou. See under Koan, the Word.

Hua-yen. Kegon, in Japanese. A School of Zen which very much valued the teachings of the Avatanshaka Sūtra (q.v.). The movement was started by Tu-shun (557–640), but definitely became a School through the work of Fa-tsang (643–712). It has also the name of Haien-shan, after a Master of that name who did much to make it more systematic. This School had ten basic principles, which were called the ten mysterious gates, used in the exposition of its philosophy of totality. Hua-yen was at first called Chien-na-p'iao-ho, which was a Chinese rendering of the word Gānda-vyūha, a portion of the Avatanshaka Sūtra.

Hui-chiao. A scholarly historian and author of Buddhist biographies up to the date of 519. Out of about 450 persons mentioned, he listed only 21 as practitioners of dhyāna.

Hui-Ke (487–593). Yeka or Eka, in Japanese. The second Chinese Zen Patriarch.

Hui-neng (638–713). Sixth and Last Chinese Patriarch of the School of Zen in China. In southern dialect his name was Wei-lang and in Japan, later, he was called Eno. His accession is described as follows.

When Hui-neng was a youth collecting firewood for a living, he happened to hear a man from the Tung Monastery (in Hupei) reciting from the Diamond Sūtra. He was so impressed with this that he made the journey of about one month to pay homage to the Head of the Monastery, who was the fifth Patriarch, named Hung-jen (Hwang Yan). He stayed in the Monastery and was given the work of splitting firewood and pounding rice. It happened that the Patriarch recognized the special capacity for satori possessed by Hui-neng, but as he was anxious not to create jealousy among his disciples, who numbered about a thousand, he spoke to him only privately and did not take further notice of him for about eight months.

When the time came for the Fifth Patriarch to consider the appointment of a successor, he invited the monks to write *gāthās* (verses), and stated that he whose verse was selected as the best would be invested with the robe and bowl which were the insignia of the Patriarch. Only one verse was written up, and that was by Shen-shiu (Shin-shau), instructor of the monks, since no other of the disciples considered himself competent. Shen-shiu felt too nervous to submit his poem direct to the Patriarch, so he wrote it on the wall of the corridor without putting his name to it. The verse was as follows:

> Our body is the Bodhi tree,
> And our mind a mirror bright.
> Carefully we wipe them hour by hour,
> And let no dust alight.

The Patriarch, having read it, said it was not good enough and invited further efforts.

It happened at this time that a young boy who read the stanza on the wall was reciting it as he passed through the rice room. Hui-neng then learnt from the boy that this stanza had been written on the wall. He recognized that it lacked enlightenment, so, with the help of the boy and a literary visitor who happened to be there, he had the following stanza composed by himself also written on the wall.

> There is no Bodhi-tree,
> Nor stand of a mirror bright.
> Since all is void,
> How can the dust alight?

47

When he saw this, the Patriarch recognized the enlightenment of the writer, and knowing it was Hui-neng, he rubbed it out in front of the monks and afterwards took an opportunity to see him at night and invest him as the Sixth Patriarch with the robe and bowl, at the same time telling him to depart from there and carry out the teaching somewhere in the south, because in that place his life would be in danger. Thus it ensued that Hui-neng taught in the temple of Fa-hsing, in the Kuang Province in the neighbourhood of Canton, which he made into a very strong centre for the doctrine of Sudden Enlightenment, saying that meditation (ting) and insight (hui) were the same. Calmness, he said, is the lamp and insight is the light, and merely sitting motionless, or even in mental introspection, is not dhyāna proper.

In the meantime Shen-shiu continued as leader in the north, and, as he was a very eloquent man and something of a politician also, he helped in the restoration of the Dynasty. When the Emperor returned after the defeat of the rebels, for which Shen-shiu had assisted in raising the necessary money, the Emperor built a new monastery for him, and he flourished greatly as teacher of the school of Gradual Enlightenment, which became for a time the orthodox sect of Buddhism in China.

It was in the south that one day Hui-neng heard some monks discussing about a flag: as to whether (a) the wind made it flap, or (b) it really did not flap because both wind and flag are really inanimate, or (c) the flapping is due to a combination of all the factors, or (d) it is only the wind that moves. Then Hui-neng said that it was not the wind, nor the flag, but their own minds that flapped. This brought him many disciples, and led to the establishment of the Southern School. Strong points in Hui-neng's teaching of meditation were 'no thought', 'no objectivity', and 'no attachment'.

The Southern School of Sudden Enlightenment near Canton, under the direction of Hui-neng, did not attract much attention outside its immediate area, until after both Shen-shiu and Hui-neng were dead. Then Shen-hui, a disciple of Hui-neng, made an effective protest against the listing of Shen-shiu as Sixth Patriarch, pointing out that Hung-jen had not made the transmission to him, but had done so to Hui-neng, having recognized his enlightenment. The result of this was that an Imperial Commission, headed by the Heir-apparent, decided to list Hui-neng as the Sixth Patriarch and Shen-hui as the 'Seventh'. The Southern School thus became well known and eventually became widely accepted in China.

Hui-neng appointed no successor to the Patriarchate, but left the Buddha-robe and the bowl with his disciple Seigen Gyoshi, with instructions to put them in the gate of the Sokei temple, Hui-neng's monastery at Sukei, near Canton.

48

In course of time Hui-neng's disciples established five schools during the Tang and Sung dynasties in the eighth to thirteenth centuries, those of Lin Chi, Tsao Tung, Yun Men, Kuei Yang and Fa Yen, named in Japanese the Rinzai, Soto, Ummon, Ikyo and Hogen. Of these five schools, the chief were the Rinzai and the Soto. (See under separate names.)

Hui-yuan (334–416). A great Chinese Scholar, disciple of Tao-an. Founder of the Amitābha or Pure Land Sect in China. He regarded meditation (dhyāna) as of the greatest importance in the religious life, as distinguished from external religious forms.

Hung-jen (605–75). Was the Fifth Patriarch in succession in the school of Zen established by Bodhidharma. The story goes that he came to the Fourth Patriarch while still a boy. When asked for his name, he said, 'Fo-hsing' (Buddha-mind). He it was who appointed Hui-neng (*q.v.*) as his successor, and handed to him the bowl and robe which had belonged to Bodhidharma, and were, as to say, his insignia of office.

Hwei-hai. Hyakujyo (*q.v.*).

Hyakujyo Nehan (720–814). A Zen Master, also known as Pai-chang Nich-p'an. Still another name for him was Hwei-hai. He founded the first Zen monasteries and laid down rules for them. He insisted on work, and was the originator of the expression: 'No work, no food.' His own book of rules was lost, but the monastic life was carried on according to them, and so a later compilation is considered to represent them quite well.

I

I Ching. There are at least three references for this word. It describes an intolerable state of doubt or tension. It is also the name of an old Chinese pilgrim, and translator of sūtras. Again, it is a name for the Chinese *Book of Changes*, a work of divination which grew up in connection with Confucianism and the Yang–yin philosophy. It was compiled over a long period, ending in the third century B.C.

Idealessness. In Zen it means not to be carried away by any particular idea in the use of mentality. (See also Wu-nien.)

I-hsuan. Lin-chi. Rinzai, in Japanese.

Ik-yo. One of the five schools of Zen in China, called also the Kuei Yang, having been founded by Kuei Shan and his disciple Yang Shan. It opposed the idea of retirement from the world, and emphasized the *infusion* of the true spirit, so that bodily life itself could become entirely enlightened and transformed. It distinguished bodily activity and 'true body', the former being the functional and the latter the essential nature. The term 'fundamental face' was also used, for that self-nature which existed before birth. It also affirmed the importance of the return from the essential nature to the functional action for the helping of the world. The Japanese name (Ik-yo) is said to have been formed from two mountains on which its monasteries were located – Isan in Hunan and Kyozan in Kiangse.

Ikyo Zen. Kuei Yang, in Chinese. A Zen sect founded by Ling Yu of Kuei Shan and Hui Chi of Yang Shan. It has now died away. It emphasized the physical forms and functions, in which by proper looking one can find the Buddha-nature which is in all.

Ingen (1592–1673). Founder of the Obaku School (*q.v.*).

Intuition. Knowledge that springs into the mind full grown from an unknown source. This is in contrast to Reason, by which knowledge is inferred from previous knowledge or perception. But all agree, it seems, that an intuition must be false if it violates reason. A reaching out for intuition is often the prior cause of an intuition, therefore intuition is not to be regarded as purely fortuitous. A good example of this is Isaac Newton's discovery of gravitation. 'Why do apples fall to the ground?' was a thwarted question of the time. Newton suddenly realized that the apples did not fall to the ground, but the apple and the ground both attracted each other. In Zen, meditation on the humblest things can give rise to most astounding intuitions, even in a moment. A bit of crumpled string or paper, or the edge of a leaf can inspire – when viewed zenically – the greatest intuitions of understanding or of beauty.

J

Japan, Buddhist Sects in. The five principal ones in Japan are usually given as Shin, Shingon, Zen, Jodo and Nichiren. Mahāyāna Buddhism was introduced into Japan in A.D. 572. At first opposed by Shinto, the old religion, it soon won the Imperial support, in the time of Prince Sjotoku Taishi (572–622). It grew rapidly in the Nara Era (710–84), having then six sects of which three – the Hosso, Kegon and Ritsu – still exist. Then came Tendai and Shingon (both 806), Yuzu Nembutsu (1123), Jodo (1174), Zen (1191), Shin (1224), and Nichiren (1253). Although 1191 is given as the date for the introduction of Zen, Dengyo Daishi, who founded the Tendai School, who had gone to China by Imperial order to study Buddhism, brought back information about Zen also earlier than that.

Ji. Ending a word, refers to a temple, as, e.g., in the word Shorin-ji.

Jinshu. Shen-shiu (*q.v.*).

Jiriki. Self-effort, which is the basis of Zen. Contrasts with tāriki.

Jodo. The Pure Land Sect (*q.v.*).

Joriki. Also called Zenjoriki. Cultivation of supernormal powers through meditation. The term is also used for the ability to respond effectively to the environment without a divided or distracted mind, which comes from the power of concentration or full attention and response without any intervening intention.

Joshu. Chao-chou (*q.v.*).

K

Kancho. Title of the priest who superintends in a Buddhist monastery or temple. Among the Rinzais he is elected, but must be a roshi.

Kanna Zen. In the twelfth century Dai Soko collected many authentic koans and arranged them into a systematic course of Zen practice, to which the name Kanna Zen was then given. The number of recognized or accepted koans in Japan is now about seven hundred.

Karma. The doctrine, taught by Buddha and also in the Hindu Scriptures, that what you do unto others will be done unto you in future incarnations, and also what you work for you will have – working including works of both body and mind, and acting including thought, speech and deed. This applies from past to present as well as from present to future, so that a man comes to birth with the character and ability, temperament and tendencies resulting from his use of these qualities and the effects of his self-culture in previous lives. The circumstances and conditions of his birth will be due to his actions in the past, towards both others and himself. This refers to the kind of body, family, wealth, etc., that he gets. But these are not regarded as binding him or forcing him to any actions. What he does in those circumstances depends upon himself – his character, will-power and perseverance, likings and love, and capacity for thought. As the conditions and circumstances result from actions in the past based upon his own past virtues and defects, they constitute appropriate opportunities for him and are to be regarded as educative, not punitive.

At birth the man will thus get a packet of karma, so to speak, and this is often called ripe karma. But he is also making new karma day by day, and paying it off day by day; this is called current or 'ready-money' karma. There is also the karma in suspense, as it were, or stored from the past, waiting for a suitable opportunity to discharge itself. This arises because some things cannot be fitted in to be repaid in the same life. It is part of the old doctrine that any good you now do goes to cancel out stored-up bad karma, which will in that case never come. Zenists usually hold to these views, just as other Buddhists do.

Some have held the view that it is not necessary to seek either enlightenment or liberation, but it is enough to cease from making new karmas, which, however, does not mean cessation from actions but the doing of actions which will cancel out old karmas, taking care not to have the kind of desires which create new ones. This opinion is not uncommon in India, and one has even come across the belief that after sages have reached liberation they must remain in incarnation until all outstanding karmic debts are paid off.

Katsu. A meaningless word, or exclamation. First used by Baso Doitsu, and later made famous by Rinzai Gigen. A striking example of it occurred at the illumination of Rinzai himself, when it was used by the Master Obaku.

Kāyas, The Three. Kāya means body or form, in Sanskrit. The three forms of a Buddha are given as follows:
Dharmakāya. The self-nature or void aspect. The real being in his true nature, indescribable and absolute.
Sambhogakāya. Body of enjoyment or realization, in which prajñā looks upwards, as it were, to the true dharma, and karuna (compassion) looks downward to the world of limitations.
Nirmānakāya. The visible human body of a Buddha in the world of forms made by mind.
Buddha, the sage of the Shākya clan (Shākyamuni) who lived circa 500 B.C. in India, is regarded as the seventh of a series of Buddhas. He prophesied that the name of the next would be Maitreya. They were all Nirmānakāyas of the one supreme and eternal Ādi-Buddha.

Kegon School. See Hua-yen.

Kensho-godo. Looking into your own nature directly and finding it to be the same as the ultimate nature of the universe. This belief is practised by the Rinzais, but ignored by the Soto Sect. It is, however, the main aim of the Daijozen, and its attainment is considered to be the real Satori. In such a satori there are degrees, that is, differences in both clarity and depth, and yet it does at first give an impression of being the whole thing.

Ke-T'eng. A word literally meaning vines and wistaria, which are entangling. It refers to the nature of koans, which are, as it were, obstructive complications, which according to some Zen Masters ought not to have been brought into Zen practice as not being of positive helpfulness.

Kleshas, The Five. A series of five human troubles or sources of trouble given in Patanjali's yoga, occasionally referred to in Zen literature. They are (1) ignorance, (2) egoism, (3 and 4) attachment and revulsion, and (5) possessiveness. In the course of overcoming these one first gives up possessiveness, then aversions, then attachments, then egoism and finally ignorance.

Koan Interview, The. On hearing the Master's bell, the student whose turn it is leaves the general meditation-hall and goes to the Master's room, after responding with two strokes on a bell to indicate that he is coming. He enters and makes his triple bow, which he will repeat on leaving. The Master gives the student a koan, and there may be quite a stormy interview, which will conclude only when the Master strikes the bell at his side.

When, later on, the student feels that he has obtained some insight from or regarding his koan, he again goes to the Master with it during the next meditation period. In the meantime what happened at the interview must be kept strictly private.

Koan, Nature of the. An exercise for the mind, beyond thought, prescribed by a Zen Master, and of such a nature that it violates the postulates of logic. It is as though one should be presented with a canvas on which many different marks had been made together at random and were asked: 'What is the meaning of this?' As there is no chance in nature, or as chance is not in the field of nature by chance, or as chance is not chance but also is not within the field of the ordinary human mind's designing, the solution of the question must be gained by 'intuition'.

All reasoning is building one thing on top of another – *adding* something to an existing and mentally seen edifice of knowledge. Then, if you are told to put in an attic underneath the cellar, you just don't know how to go about it. But if the person who told you to do it were the Supreme Architect of the Universe, or it were your Zen Master – which comes to the same thing if you be facing your Master with true Zen faith – you try, and you *go on trying* until suddenly you have solved the problem.

It is the way of nature. That primitive creature who first developed an eye, beginning first with a spot on the skin more sensitive than the rest of the skin, and later ending with our present visual organ, did so by trying to see, even though it did not know beforehand what seeing was, nor even thought what it was doing. It was the will to live that was the impulse behind the trying, so psychologically we may say that the mind is baffled by the koan, but the life goes on and, further, in the case of the Zen pupil, it goes on voluntarily: his life is in his will and his will is his Zen faith and he does not give up.

In an experiment with a monkey and a mirror the ingredients were a pet or tame monkey belonging to the lady of the house, a long thin chain ending in a belt round the monkey's waist, and a tall cheval mirror. The monkey was tethered near the mirror and the lady, with her husband, watched. The monkey caught sight of the image, grimaced at it and tried to catch hold of it. Frustrated in that, it dashed round to the back of the mirror several times with increasing speed. Again frustrated, it came close to the mirror and reached an arm round to try to get hold of 'that other monkey' while it could still be seen from the front of the glass. Failing in that, the monkey soon gave up and took no further interest in the matter. The difference between the monkey and the monk is that the monk does not give up. He will discover the mirror – in this case the *no-mirror*. (See under Mirror.)

Here we see why it must be a Zen Master who sets the problem. It must come out of the depths of his Master-mind, which for the present is super-mind to the pupil – and as such 'no-mind', being not of the nature of mind (as between subject and object), and perhaps even the nature of Buddha-mind. It is not that the Zen Master concocts or thinks out or plans the statement which is the koan. From him the situation is spontaneous, because at the time of expressing it he is in his Buddha-nature and it is from that that the koan springs forth. It is much as in sitting with a psychiatrist: the patient must respond to a series of words instantly, and without thought or hesitation, and only such answers as are without hesitation (that is, without thought) will be useful to the doctor in his diagnosis. There is this difference, however, that the patient's responses come out of his sub-mind, as we may call it, and the Master's koan comes out of his super-mind.

This is the reason (often unseen as such) why in the Zen monasteries koans of Masters have been collected and are used over and over again and prescribed, often as a definite series or course. Is it not for the same reason that musicians play the classical pieces over and over again, that the 'beauty' of the compositions as known to the original composer may become more known to the players or to the audience, either or both?

In a secondary way the koan is a kind of test of the inquirer's enlightenment, since he may or may not 'catch on', and show in some way that the koan has had immediate effect.

Koan, The Word. In Chinese, kung-an. At first the word hua-tou was much used. This means 'ends', as in the end or purpose of a sentence, or the critical or significant word in a question, such as 'Who?' which determines the aim. The supreme hua-tou is the word 'wu', which occurred when someone asked Joshu whether a dog has Buddha-nature, and he answered merely, 'wu'. If that is a statement it is also a question (however obscure) for the pupil; for example, 'What is nothing (wu)?' 'It is no "what"'. 'What then?' And so on, continuing the meditation on wu until, at the moment of illumination the ideas of question and answer are both lost. The koans in actual

56

use by Zen Masters are very numerous (1700 are alluded to) and varied. Some Masters have classified them into five or more groups. Although there are so many koans, it is possible to attain satori by the proper 'solution' of only one.

The word kung-an originally referred to a document relating to an official transaction, and so was adopted into Zen as meaning a specific item scheduled for attention or 'before the house', or 'on the agenda'.

Koans, Answers to. Hakuin classified the different kinds of answers traditionally connected with the standard koans, such as (1) Hosshin, by repeating the Master's words, gestures, actions or even silence in a way which shows that the pupil has 'caught on'; (2) Kikan, by an action or the use of some handy object; (3) Gonsen, by a short talk, referring to something concrete, but free from thoughts or abstractions; (4) Nento, by a reply difficult to grasp because seemingly quite unconnected; (5) Goi, referring to the five relations and non-relations of the absolute and the relative. There are also some more, mostly for the very advanced students, such as Jujukin, relating to daily life; Kido-no-daibetsu, Kido's answers to his selected hundred koans, and Matsugo-no-rokan, a koan made by a Zen Master for finally testing his own most advanced students.

Koans, Examples of. Koans have usually issued from Zen Masters at the conclusion of a brief dialogue between Master and pupil or inquirer-in-the-status-of-pupil, or else simply in response to a question. The following are classical examples:

Question: 'Who is Buddha?'
Answer: 'Three measures of flax.'
Question: 'What is the meaning of Buddha's coming from the West?'
Answer: 'The cypress tree in the courtyard.'
Question: 'Does a dog have the Buddha-nature?'
Answer: 'Nothing (wu)'.
Question: 'What is the body of space?'
Answer: 'Your old teacher is underneath your feet.'
Question: 'What is Buddha?'
Answer: 'The cat is climbing the post.'
Sometimes it was the Master who put the question; for example:
'Who is it who calls on the name of Buddha?'
'What is the sound of the clap of one hand?'
'A man is hanging over an abyss by his teeth. Someone asks him why Bodhidharma came to China. If he does not answer he fails. If he does answer he falls. What should he do?'
'A buffalo leaves its enclosure on the edge of an abyss. Horns, head and hoofs pass through. Why cannot his tail also pass?'

Kobo Daishi or Kukai. Founder of the Shingon Sect in Japan (*q.v.*).

Kufu. Naturalness in bodily action, which comes about when the mind allows the body the full harmony of its own co-ordinations by not concentrating on a particular part of the body. (See under Arts of Zen.) It does not preclude bodily training, as that is desirable so that all the muscles and nerves related to a given form of skill may become properly and proportionately developed.

When performing an action the thought of oneself with self-motive often stands in the way of the perfect action. This applies to swordsmanship, archery and indeed all the arts. It also applies to meditation and literary pursuits: there was an author and lecturer who said that in the course of writing or of speaking, or afterwards, he would sometimes 'come to' and realize with some surprise that it was *he* who was doing it or had done it. There is no doubt that it was while not thinking of himself that he did his best work, but it must also be noted that he had plenty of practice behind him. To go into this impersonal condition at will is part of Zen. The self here deprecated is, of course, the personally built-up picture of self, or self-image, not the pure consciousness of self. (See under Self.)

Kumārajīva. An Indian Buddhist who went to China A.D. 401 and founded the Middle Doctrine school. He translated many Buddhist texts into Chinese, and also made explanatory comments, with the aid of about eight hundred monks, whom he organized into a translation bureau. Scholars by the thousand flocked to him from all over China. He supported and made definite the doctrine of the Void.

Kundokuho. The Japanese mode of reading Chinese writing.

K'ung. Shūnyatā (*q.v.*) or emptiness.

Kwan. An exclamation often used by Ummon.

Kwatz. In Chinese, He (pronounced Hay). A meaningless word often used by Rinzai, sometimes in a sentence, sometimes by itself, as an exclamation or shout. For example, once Rinzai asked a disciple whether striking with a stick or exclaiming 'Kwatz' conveyed or awakened more truth. When the pupil answered, 'Neither', and on being further pressed exclaimed 'Kwatz!' Rinzai struck him with a stick. This, no doubt (in our opinion), simply knocked the disciple off his mental perch, for he definitely had been mentalizing.

Rinzai had what appeared to be four degrees of force in using the shout. He did not describe them as degrees, but as (1) like Vajrarāja's sacred sword, cutting the chain of thought; (2) like a crouching golden-haired lion, to scare the deluded; (3) like the noise made by a vibrating reed, or sounding-rod, to probe deep into the inquirer's understanding, and (4) not a vocal shout, but a kind of blast of awakening to reality. The use of this shout originated with Baso. When he launched it at one of his disciples, Hyakujo, it deafened him for three days, according to one story.

Sometimes Rinzai resorted to violence without the use of a stick. It is recorded that once, when a monk named Jo asked him about the fundamental principle of Buddhism, he got up and gave him a slap. Another monk reminded Jo that he should then bow to the Master; in doing so, it is said, he suddenly realized the essential truth. Rahuko, a disciple of Rinzai, preferred the use of the stick.

Kyogen Chickan. A disciple of Isan, well known from his being the source of the broken-tile 'koan'. This arose when he was doing some raking work. He had been puzzling for a long time about enlightenment, when it happened that his rake struck a broken tile with a startling sound. Suddenly he experienced Satori. No one can say what the 'association' was that produced this effect; consistent Zenists would probably say that it was no association of ideas or revived experience, but was due to a cessation of current or habitual mentalizing, which permitted the new experience, which was a perfectly natural and even in a sense ordinary fact of our being, but had been obscured by desires and thoughts – as some would say 'Like clouds and the sun'. This is also in agreement with the idea of illumination being 'the original countenance before birth', which arose in the Ikyo school.

Another historical incident occurred in connection with Kyogen. It was on an occasion when the Master Kyozan was talking with him that he came out with the distinction between Tathāgata Zen (nyorai in Japanese) and Patriarchal Zen (soshi in Japanese), satori being identified with the latter, and the Tathāgata Zen being the teaching obtained from the Lankāvatāra Sūtra.

L

Lamp and Light. One of Hui-neng's favourite similes, to illustrate unity. He said that the lamp is the 'body' for the light, and the light is the 'use' of the lamp, and pointed out that dhyāna (meditation) and prajñā (wisdom) are similarly related. To understand this one must remember that meditation is not withdrawal. The correction which dhyāna brings in, which is called shunyatā (emptiness), refers to the seeing of the self-nature as empty of all that is found in other-nature. It is not to be confused with the Hindu theory of māyā, as it has no reference to the production of forms and ideas (comparisons of forms and their relationships or doings).

As regards dhyāna and prajñā, Shen-hui (the Seventh Patriarch) expressed the teaching of the Nirvāna Sūtra in saying that when dhyāna exceeds prajñā there is bound to be more ignorance, and when prajñā exceeds dhyāna there will be erroneous views, but when they are equal there will be seeing into the Buddha-nature.

This is a way of saying that dhyāna is truly dhyāna and prajñā truly prajñā only when the two are together. Ta-chu-Hui-hai, a disciple of Ma-tsu, said that when they are together it is all dhyāna and all prajñā, and there is then Liberation (*q.v.*).

Lankāvatāra Sūtra. This scripture was already in China about the first century A.D., and it was taken up especially by Bodhidharma because it presented so strongly the essential principles of Zen and the nature of Buddha's enlightenment. Bodhidharma passed it on to his successor for these reasons. The first translation into Chinese was made about A.D. 440. There were two other and easier translations, made later.

The Lankāvatāra Sūtra has the peculiar character of being a quite unsystematic series of notes, full of philosophy of the 'essence of mind'. It is especially difficult because of its brevity of expression.

It did not, however, continue in favour, being too Indian for the Chinese mind, which has a bent more practical than philosophical, even in its pursuit of the unseen or unknown.

Lao-tsu. Author of the famous book *Tao Te Ching* (*q.v.*), and, as such, the accredited 'founder' of Taoism. His date is generally given as the fourth century B.C. According to the book of Historical Records (Shih Chi), his occupation was that of custodian of documents or archives of the State of Chau. It is related that Confucius, the great teacher of social order and duty, came to consult him on the subject of rituals, and also asked his advice. Lao-tsu told him that all these things did not add to the real value of any man. Afterwards Confucius told his students that he understood the nature and uses of most things, but he found Lao-tsu as difficult to understand as the Dragon that goes to heaven on winds and clouds. Ultimately Lao-tsu decided to leave the State. The officer at the border post, named Yin-hi, begged him not to go away without writing a book. So he dictated the *Tao-te-ching*, a small book containing only about five thousand written characters.

Liberation. Freedom from the rounds of births and deaths is sought in all schools of Buddhism. Inasmuch, however, as aversion from objects and persons (dwesha) is as binding as attachment to them (rāga), both being desires or thirsts (trishnā or tanhā), the desire for escape would thwart itself. The Zenist, however, avoids this, because he aims only at illumination or satori, disregarding the wheel of births and deaths, although it is understood by all that enlightenment automatically cancels the desires which cause rebirth and so brings the process to an end. (See also under Lamp and Light.)

Lin-chi. Also I hsuan, Rinzai, in Japanese (d. 867). Founder of the Lin-chi or Rinzai sect (*q.v.*). Noted personally for his violent howling, shouting and beating methods, which apparently were based not on emotional outbursts, but developed as a psychological form of pedagogy.

Lin-chi had a fourfold system for snatching away his students' attachments to subjects and objects. The first part of the process was removing the subject and keeping the object, next removing the object and keeping the subject, then removing both subject and object, and, fourthly, keeping both subject and object. To illustrate these – on being questioned by Chih-i (K'e Fu) – he recited the following four statements:

(1) 'On a warm day the fields are carpeted with flowers; the white hair of a baby is hanging down like silk.' In this there is no subject.

(2) 'Now that the royal writ runs throughout the land, the commander, free from the smoke of battle, goes abroad.' In this there is no object.

(3) 'Isolation is complete when all communications have been cut.' In this there is neither subject nor object.

(4) 'While the king ascends his precious throne, old peasants sing their songs.' In this there is both subject and object.

These four are as translated by Lu Kuan in his *Ch'an and Zen Teaching*, Series Two. They give us a clue to 'the Chinese mind', with its preference for thing or picture, not word, such that even when words are used the statement is a picture.

Lin-Chi Zen Sect. Rinzai, in Japanese. Founded in China by I-hsuan of Lin Chi. (See under Rinzai and Sudden School.)

Logic. Zen practice does not work with logic, but rather with perception, on which all logic ultimately depends. After all, the major premiss in a logical statement is based upon an 'if'. For example, 'All men have brains; Mr Jones is a man; therefore Mr Jones must have a brain.' But how do we know that all men have brains? We have not examined them all. 'The sun rises every day; therefore it will rise tomorrow.' But how does one know that the sun rises every day? One has not seen every day. Perhaps it would be more modest of the logician if he were to word it, 'If all men have brains, which is the fact in all the cases known to us, then as Mr Jones is a man he should have a brain.'

The Zenist will not accept such unfounded knowledge, especially in exploratory search, such as that of seeking to know the self-nature. Everything must be discovered by the direct method. So when a question, 'Where is emptiness?' came up, the Zen Master Fu-ch'i said: 'It is like a Persian tasting red pepper.'

Lion Koan, The. A well-known koan. Yakusen asked Ungan if he played with a lion, and, on receiving an affirmative, asked how many, to which the answer was six. Then Ungan said that he too could play with a lion, but only one. Then said Ungan, 'One is six and six is one.'

This is a good problem, since meditate upon it as long as he will and as fruitfully as is possible for the human mind, the thinker will be baffled in the end. He will find a flaw in every interpretation. But if he persists, new light will arise, even up to the satori experience, because, as his mind has failed (fundamentally and by its very nature) but his will has gone on, some newness of the man will sprout, revealing to him an aspect of life of which he has not been consciously aware. This new aspect gives tranquillity and joy.

Modern students may see in this and other such stories a reasonable analogy. From the inadequacy of sensations, emotions arose; from the inadequacy of emotions mentality arose; from the inadequacy of mentality ethical impulses arose; and – says religion – from the inadequacy of human love the vision of the divine love can arise. The koan is thus natural, but whether a person can apply it practically seems to depend upon his competence, and perhaps even more upon his insistence and persistence. In many cases the person is inadequate to the koan. Perhaps that is why so many persons need so many koans – for the sake of practice, developing their insistence and persistence. Otherwise, one would be sufficient.

tus School. See under Tendai and Saddharma-pundarīka.

yang. Capital town of Wei, on the Yellow river (Hoang Ho), in northern China, a great centre of Buddhist study and activity to which many monks from India had come, bringing numerous manuscripts. This was the situation when Bodhidharma (*q.v.*) came there after his unprofitable interview with the Emperor Wu-ti. As Bodhidharma, with his emphasis on the seeking of the Buddha-mind, was not welcomed there he left and made his way to the Shorin Temple on Mount Su (Sung Shan), also called the Wu-tai Mountain.

M

Mādhyamika School. See under Mahāyāna and Kumārajīva.

Mahākāshyapa. Name of one of Buddha's immediate disciples, who was the first to catch from the Teacher the unspoken knowledge obtainable and transmissable only in the Zen manner.

Mahāprajnā Pāramitā Sūtra, The. A scripture dealing very deeply with emptiness, form, sensation, perception, etc., much valued for zenic meditation. It is full of those paradoxes which lead to release from limited conceptions, and thus help the aspirant to 'reach the other shore'.

The heart (hridaya) section of it ends in a triumphal utterance: 'Gate, gate, paragate, para-sangate, bodhi, swāhā.' This has been freely translated in Dwight Goddard's *Buddhist Bible* as follows: 'Gone, gone, gone to that other shore, O Prajnāpāramitā! So mote it be.' Gate has to do with something or someone 'gone'; para means 'other' or 'beyond'. The prefix san added to gate indicates a uniting – thus 'gone into union with beyond.' Bodhi (wisdom or perfect knowledge) is here taken as the Prajnāpāramitā. Swāhā is a word used at the end of an offering, somewhat as 'So be it!' or 'Amen!' or 'Om!' Reaching 'the other shore' is a figure of speech used by Buddha to signify the attainment of illumination or nirvāna.

Mahāyāna Buddhism. The Zen movement is usually regarded as a part of Mahāyāna Buddhism, which arose as a reform movement at the time of the Second Buddhist Council, about 383 B.C. At the First Council, which was held shortly after Buddha's death (about 483 B.C.), an accepted collection of scriptures has been made, in which Ananda had been the chief reciter of teaching (dhamma), and Upali the principal rememberer of sermons on conduct, discipline and monastic rules (vinaya). The Second Council (about 383 B.C.) was called for the purpose of eliminating some unauthorized practices. At the same time, however, a rival meeting was called by a group of 10,000, called the Mahāsanghikas, to oppose the orthodox Elders, whose teaching came to be called the Theravāda (Doctrine of the Elders).

At a Third Council, held about 240 B.C., a third collection of scriptures and commentaries, mostly metaphysical and psychological, was added so that by then there were three 'baskets' (pitaka) of them – the Dhamma (law or teachings), Vinaya (conduct) and Abhidhamma. The Tripitika collection contains 65,000 books, of which some 7,000 were translated into Chinese by the tenth century.

Meantime the other movement grew stronger, so that by about A.D. 70 the Mahāyāna (Great Path) doctrine was definitely being formed, with commentaries on the three 'baskets' and other additions, using now the Sanskrit language instead of the Pali, which was used before that.

Of the two main streams of Mahāyāna which were formed one became the Yogāchāra School, founded by Asanga (410–500 A.D.), assisted by his brother Vasubandhu. This has been called the Idealistic School, because of its 'mind-only' doctrine, declaring that the mind (manas), as coordinator of the senses, with its 'store-consciousness' (ālaya), is the source of all things (characteristics, dharmas). This is what gives the nature or character (thusness, tathatā) to all things, as a sort of noumenon for them, thus avoiding the idea that they have any reality of their own. Equally, it goes against a void (shūnyatā). The influence of this school of Mahāyāna reached China when Paramārtha (q.v.) went there and translated the principal scriptures into Chinese. From that work arose the She-lun School, which merged into the Fa-hsiang (Hosso, q.v.) School founded by Hsuan-tsang (q.v.).

The other main school of Mahāyāna, called the Middle Doctrine School (Mādhyamika), started by Nāgārjua (A.D. 100–200), upheld the idea of the Void (shūnyatā, q.v.). It draws a distinction between the relatively or phenomenally real, produced by causation, with no independent reality. The higher truth then is that only the Void is really real, or independently real, and this involves eight negations or denials – no production and no extinction, no annihilation and no permanence, no unity and no diversity, no coming and no going. There must be a middle *without extremes* between each of these pairs, which is thus an Absolute Middle, and this is the Void, or Nirvāna. While the Void is relatively or at first the denial of the extremes, it later is seen (in deeper meditation) as the nature of the All, and the extremes mentioned and in fact all dharmas are, as it were, deductions from this by which the really real is veiled. This School of thought was carried to China by Kumārajīva (q.v.), and then developed by Chi-tsang. It was after Ashwaghosha (q.v.), about A.D. 100, that the name Mahāyāna began to be used.

It was from these sources that the teachings favoured by the early Ch'anists of China arose. The Schools in China which emphasized meditation (dhyāna in Sanskrit, ch'an in Chinese, and zen in Japanese) blended their purposes and ideas with those of the Tao (q.v.), with the result that Ch'an, and later Zen, came to mean that kind of meditation which is specially aimed at the Tao and the Buddha-mind or Buddha-nature (*q.v.*).

Makyo. Extra-sensory perceptions which may occur in some cases in the early states of meditation. As being at best phenomenal, these are not encouraged by the Zenist.

Ma-tsu (d. 788). Also called Tao-i, Ma-chu and Baso. The great advancement of Zen after Hui-neng was largely due to the brilliance of this Master, who tutored as many as eighty full Masters. He was the originator of the method of the koan, in the ninth century. His successor was Nan-chuan. He was a disciple of Huai-jang, a disciple of Hui-neng. Hwei-hai (Hyakujyo), the first Zen monastery-founder, was a disciple of Ma-tsu.

Māyā. An old Hindu, and especially Vedantic teaching, referring to the creation of all manifest things, of both the mind and the body, from ignorance (avidyā), through the two processes of (1) veiling (āvarana) the reality, and then (2) building on the basis of the veiling by projection (vikshepa). The product – the whole world of body and mind – is then called a māyā. The word māyā is often translated 'illusion', which is not to be confused with 'delusion'. Strictly, in modern terms, it seems very closely related to the idea of relativity or relative truth, which is never *really* correct. (See under Creation.)

Mayoi. The state of doubt or uncertainty, as contrasted with satori. Sometimes this 'mayoi' is translated as discrimination, understood in the sense of comparison of things with reference to their similarities and differences, not in the Vedantic sense of distinguishing the real self from all the erroneous self-images, or ideas of self. The word mayoi means standing at a crossroad and being in doubt (vikalpa in Sanskrit) as to which way to go. This is the result of relying upon 'the ten thousand things' (the Chinese way of alluding to the world of various objects) for guidance or knowledge. In the transfer of attention from the ten thousand things to the mirror itself, there is definitely, Hui-neng insists, no gradation. The transit must be sudden.

Meditation. Although Zen is sometimes described in the West as the Meditation School of Buddhism, it is not in its present form strictly Buddhistic, and it certainly is not a passive meditation, as the word so often implies in the West. Nor, incidentally, is the Hindu meditation prescribed in the Yoga Sutras by Patanjali passive. But there is in both East and West so much so-called meditation which is nothing but poising the mind on a concept or on an object that it is necessary to state here that Zen meditation is a strenuous task of consciousness, whether it takes the form of a temporary or a periodical effort, or aims at being a constant background in the midst of other material and mental activities.

These remarks apply to both the Soto and the Rinzai schools of Zen, which differ in that the Soto method aims at observing one's own mind in tranquillity, also called serene reflection (mo-chao), or the quietness of no-thought (wu-nien), while the Rinzai gives the student's mind a hard task usually involving violent or at least vigorous treatment of a koan problem, or even a physically startling shout or blow which can knock the mind-process 'off its perch'.

Reflection or meditation is, however, not in either case a *suppression* of thoughts or of knowledge of facts, but a complete response to them, and thus a discovery of the limits of the mind, coupled with a will to live or reach beyond – not, however, with a thought of 'beyond', but just going on. Thus has arisen the idea that it is ultimately 'a leap in the dark', or perhaps into the dark.

Meditation, Two forms of. Two forms of meditation are clearly distinguishable in Zen practice. One may be called the outward-going; the other the inward-going. Both of them are upward-going, insomuch as the aim in both cases is the prajñā, the realization of the Buddha-mind, involving the principles of 'no-mind', 'emptiness', and 'suchness'. On the whole the inward-going is the preferred method of the Rinzai schools, which aim to realize one's own Buddha-mind, while the outward-going is the preferred method of the Soto.

This distinction can be understood by reference to the latter part of the dialogue of the cat and the post koan (see under Koans, Examples of). In that story, after the inquirer asked, 'What is Buddha?' and the Master answered, 'The cat is climbing the post,' the hearer wanted further elucidation, but the Master only said: 'Go and ask the post.' The truth is that everything has the Buddha-nature, and there it can be found.

It would, of course, be quite unzenic to interpret this as a parable, or an allegory, or as an analogy, or even as a rebuff to a foolish question. In principle, however, all things tell us what they are, though it be through our senses, such as they may be. As all things have the Buddha nature, any picture in the mind or object in the world can be used to find it. The cat and post is one of these which would be very vivid to the ordinary person; meditation upon this with the refusal to accept its personality-picture as the true self-nature of it, if persisted in without diminution of the vivid quality of consciousness which the familiarity with it makes possible, must end in the perception of the true identity of it, including its Buddha-nature. The clue to success in meditation of this kind is non-diminution.

We may, indeed, realize that here also applies the method of meditation defined by Patanjali, in which there is first the concentration on something until it is very clear and the conscious attention is at its best as regards quality; then, secondly, there is a flow of the mind-effort without diminution of that quality; and then a culmination which comes when the mental seeing of it (comparisons: differences and resemblances) ceases. Patanjali called the third part of this process samādhi.

The principle of the Cat and Post Mondo is easily seen in many other statements by which Zen Masters have directed the meditations of students. A few such were:

'The green bamboos are swaying in the wind; the cold pine trees are shivering in the moonlight.'

'The white cow is lying by the cool stream in the open field.'

'Do you hear the murmuring sound of the mountain stream? That is the way to Zen.'

Sometimes verses of poetry have been written which are of this character. Indeed, it may be said that poetry in general conveys much more than prose because of the pauses or poises in thought which it causes. (See also under Za-Zen and Poetry.)

Middle Doctrine School. See under Mahāyāna.

Mind. The word is used in several senses in Zen. There is the Buddha-mind, which is not thinking and its thoughts. The ordinary mind is objective, even when abstract, since it is *seen* within, which involves a duality of seer and seen. Looking into one's own mind is quite similar to looking into a mirror. It is not so with the Buddha-mind; in that case we have pure consciousness knowing pure consciousness (prajñā, not vijñā). The Buddha-mind is always present, and we always know it, but not by thoughts, still less by desire. (See under Worlds, the Three.)

Mind, Going beyond. Defined as intellect, mind is to be transcended in Zen. Or perhaps it would be more accurate to say it is to be set aside. Knowing is not to be confused with thinking. Even in the use of the senses there is no meditation or thought-process; for example, in seeing red there is knowing but not thinking. So, even when the Zenist sets aside thinking about something, he is still aiming at knowing it. Even then the knower cannot convey his knowledge as it is, just as one who sees red colour cannot convey his knowledge of it to one who has never seen it.

The psychology of the knowing is not a matter of interest to the strict Zenist, who works only on the attainment of the knowledge, direct. But others may reason that the method of Zen is logical, because of the doctrine of the unity of composites. For example, a really good picture by a competent artist contains no single stroke on the canvas which is not essential to the effect. There is nothing that can be left out, and nothing more that can be put in if the picture is perfect, and then the observer has to absorb the whole picture in one act of vision to get the artist's idea. The same applies to music, and in fact all the forms of direct vision, as distinguished from thought or inference and from information conveyed by words or gestures.

Mirror. A man can rightly be called a mirror of the universe, since all things can be reflected in his mind, but the universe cannot be called a mirror for man, since nothing that he sees in it can show him what he is. (See also under Hui-neng.) The following also bears on this subject:

> To prove they aren't nobodies
> Men resort to externals.
> Could anything be more comical?
> Then there is the ostentatious neglect of externals.

Mirror, Gāthā of the. Very clearly expressed by Shen-shiu, learned director of studies under the Fifth Patriarch, in the verse which he wrote on the temple wall, as follows:

> Our body is the Bodhi-tree,
> And our mind a mirror bright.
> Carefully we wipe them hour by hour,
> And let no dust alight.

This was challenged by Hui-neng, who wrote beside it the following verse:

> There is no Bodhi-tree,
> Nor stand of a mirror bright.
> Since all is void,
> Where can the dust alight?

The zenic correctness of Hui-neng's gāthā lies in that it shows the mind to be inexpressible and the path not a matter of cultivation. It indicates that in Zen there is only 'statement by non-statement' and 'cultivation by non-cultivation'. (See also under Hui-neng, Ma-tsu, self-nature, no-mind, etc.)

Monasteries. Zen monasteries as such were first founded by Hyakujyo (q.v.). They are more in the nature of schools than places of worship, and all through the ninth and tenth centuries they had no rituals or ceremonies, but later, with more popularity and their becoming publicly supported institutions, the old rituals were expected and were introduced. (See also under Zendo, Angya, Sesshin, etc.)

Monasteries, Food in. The food given in the Zen monasteries is very simple. Breakfast consists of gruel and pickled vegetables; lunch has rice, barley, soup and pickles; supper repeats the breakfast. If, however, a monk is invited to the home of a patron he may partake of a sumptuous meal. During meals, which are preceded and ended by certain recitations, quietness is the rule. Before commencing to eat, the monk puts out on the side a small portion of the food as a sort of offering. After the meal the monk washes his small bowls in his large bowl, which is filled with hot water by an attendant, who also takes away the dirty water in a bucket which he carries round. When finished, they all rise and go out together.

The recitations before meals include the Hridaya Sūtra of the Mahāprajñā-pāramitā, the names of the Buddha, and five meditations on topics concerning personal conduct and character, and the fact that the food is being taken to sustain the body in its pursuit of zenic attainment for the benefit of all beings.

Though meals are taken three times a day, only the midday meal is formal. The breakfast is sometimes called 'ceiling gruel', because a reflection of the ceiling can be seen in it, as it is so watery. The evening repast is for some reason called 'medicinal'. Eating at other times is strictly forbidden. The meals are eaten in silence, all must try to finish at the same time, and there must be no waste, not even a drop of water. Monks are all vegetarians, and they abstain from liquor.

Monasteries, Running Exercises in. In some Zen monasteries the running exercise is still carried on. At a signal from the director the monks rise after an hour's meditation and run rapidly round the hall in a circle, following one another. In this they are told to keep their heads up and their eyes in front. At a given signal from the director they all stand perfectly still and then sit down again and proceed with their meditation. Sometimes there is only walking, and then they go quietly in single file with the hands on the chest, one over the other.

Monasteries, Work in. Zen monks all work, including the Master. The monasteries own land, which is enough to support them, through the farming work done by the monks. Things which are needed, but cannot be provided by work on this land are obtained through voluntary gifts in money or kind by the Zen laity. They keep the monastery clean, look after the grounds and gardens, raise vegetables, cut firewood, etc. In the autumn they often go out with hand-carts to pick up the vegetables, etc., left in the fields as not good enough for marketing. Collecting food from donors is also one of their tasks.

To these monks the daily duties of life, in the fields, or in the housework of the monasteries, including cooking, appear as matters of training just as spiritual, so to say, as any work or service in the temple itself.

This applies also to the life of the female monks in the 'convents', and to those who are in monasteries where they share the temple with men, though in those they reside in separate living quarters. These female monks or nuns have shaven heads and wear the same clothing as the men. In all cases there is a strict regimen and no laziness or egotism is permitted.

Mondo. Wen-ta, in Chinese. This is a question-and-answer system that differs from the koan in that an immediate answer is demanded. Here there is no continued wrestling, as it were, in terrible unmental attentiveness, as in the case of the koan. An immediate answer is required, without thought. It will be noticed that this is another way of side-stepping the thought process while maintaining the attentiveness. For example, a Zen Master once held out a stick and said, 'Call it not a stick; if you do you assert. Nor deny that it is a stick; if you do, you negate. Without affirmation or denial, speak, speak!' The answers can be quite revealing, and psychologically cleansing, provided they are not interpreted.

Mokusho Zen. Another name for the Mokushu or quiet sitting in Za-Zen favoured by the Soto Sect.

Monkeys, The Six. Someone once asked Chung Hueng-en how to look into one's self-nature. Suppose, he replied, that there is a cage with six windows, in which there is a monkey. Someone calls at one window, 'O monkey,' and he responds. Someone else calls at another window, and again he responds. And so on.

Mu. In Chinese, wu (q.v.). An expression of negation.

Mumonkan. Wu-men-kuan, in Chinese. A collection of forty-eight Chinese koans made by Mumon Ekai in the thirteenth century. Translated in English, the name means, 'The Pass without a Gate'.

Mushinjo. Certain meditation practices which do not lead to satori. Particularly Bombuzen, Gedozen and Shojo Zen (q.v.). It is also used in reference to a state of self-induced trance, lasting perhaps for hours or days, not to be confused with satori.

Myoshinji. A famous Rinzai monastery of Kyoto, former capital of Japan.

Mysticism. To describe Zen illumination as a sort of mysticism would be disapproved by Zenists, because as ordinarily understood mysticism is the vision of a reality beyond the world of the senses and the mind. It is of course true that some mystics consider that their illumination lies not in the perception or realization of something beyond this world, but only of the real nature of it, as distinguished from their previous wrong view and wrong understanding. In such cases the Zen experience could be called a sort of mysticism. The Zen experience should also result in seeing with the eyes open as well as closed, and the Zen way of seeing should come to be the only way of seeing for the Zen Master, at all times and in all places, and should apply to all the senses, not merely to seeing.

N

Nāgārjuna. Famous Indian Buddhist philosopher, founder of the Mādhyamika School. (See under Mahāyāna.)

Nāmarūpa. One of the Nidānas (*q.v.*).

Nan-ch'uan. Nansen, in Japanese (748–834). A disciple of Ma-tsu. Noted especially for his sayings on the subject of Tao:

'The ordinary mind is Tao.'

'Tao is beyond both knowing and not-knowing.'

'When one tries to attain Tao one deviates from it.'

'When one attains to Tao one will see it clearly.'

Nangaku Ejo. Disciple of Hui-neng. It is related that, when they first met, the Patriarch asked him where he came from, and was told, 'I came from Mount Sū.' Hui-neng then asked him what sort of a thing that was which came, and Nangaku Ejo replied that he was not at all a sort of a thing. This was deeply significant, and indeed revealing. It may be compared to a similar incident which occurred in India when Dr Paul Brunton went to see the Maharishi Ramana in South India. Dr Brunton, when asked what he had come for, said 'I want to know –' 'What is this "I" that wants to know?' demanded the Maharishi.

Nansen. Nan-ch'uan (*q.v.*).

Naturalness. The expressions 'natural' and 'according to Nature' are often used by Zenists. They do not regard Nature and man as opponents. In this matter they would be generally inclined rather to the Western proposition that 'nature is conquered by obedience', except that the word conquered strikes a somewhat jarring note.

All creatures adapt themselves (their own bodies) to their environment. As Jennings, the famous naturalist, put it, the seal did not take to the water because it had flappers, but grew flappers because it took to the water. Why did seals not grow flappers in *addition* to legs? Because it is easier to modify what one has than to grow new limbs. Similarly, birds, the fliers, have two wings and two legs instead of two wings and four legs. Men as former tree-dwellers developed two arms in place of two forelegs, not in addition to four legs. Similarly, it is easy to see, when man came down from his trees, and assumed an upright posture for convenience in the use of his arms he started to balance himself on two legs by walking on his hocks, which has proved a far from ideal arrangement as the lack of springs at that joint tend to jar his spine.

In Nature, man cooperates with materials and objects by knowing them and by making alliance with them; for example, he joins with iron, respecting the nature of iron, when he makes knives and iron ploughs. So as regards his body it is wisdom for man to accept it as it has grown, as its forms have been handed along by the habit-system called heredity. So he rests, works and nourishes the body 'according to Nature' – *its* nature, that is, except when his mentality tells him to make some slight bodily adaptation to a particular purpose.

All these ideas, although they express discoveries of modern evolutionary science unknown to the old Zen Masters, are nevertheless in agreement with their *feeling* of relation to Nature, as far as the body and mind are concerned. The self-nature (*q.v.*) of the Zenist is, however, overlooked or ignored by modern science, and often, if studied (perhaps under the term 'spirit' or 'self' by the religious or the philosophic), is regarded as not of the same natural world as body and mind. This the consistent Zenist will not allow. The self-nature of everything is fundamentally the same, in his eyes. He seeks to know it, and he feels that obedience to it and acceptance of it are wisdom, and lead to happiness or joy.

It is to be noted that to the Zenist naturalness does not mean following bodily inclinations without judgement and restraint. Proper time, place, quantity, frequency and all the rest are to be consulted. There is very much in modern life which is far out of natural balance, owing to modern public education or indoctrination, especially by advertising and by sensational literature, which promote excessive and unnatural eating and sex. So 'Be natural' does not imply 'Do what you feel like at the moment; obey your impulses and desires,' but first be a man, a thinker, and second, discover the whole of your nature, and especially that essential self-nature which most people overlook.

When Zenists speak of naturalness, they have behind them an immense Buddhistic and Taoistic tradition, including certain beliefs, self-disciplines, especially ethical, such as the right mode of living in business as well as private life. The spontancity of the Zenist respects all these as being not rules and regulations but the proper nature of man. So there is no suggestion of indulgence or yielding to perverted promptings from others or from outgrown impulses.

Nature, The Teacher. 'It is nature alone that teaches us about itself' is good Zen doctrine. Only red can tell us what red is; no man can do so. Only a cow can tell us what a cow is. Only a mountain can tell us what a mountain is. 'And what of myself, how can I come to know myself?' Only the self can tell you what the self is. So, look at the self. 'But how can I look at the self, since it is not an object of sense?' The answer to that was given by Buddha. When you touch the ground with your foot you feel, or should feel, two things – the ground and the foot. When you think of a cow you should be aware of the cow *and the thought*. If you are not aware of the thought as well as the cow, how will you know you are thinking and not seeing?

In that case, you could be in a state of delusion. The pressure of the thought on the cow and of the cow on the thought – both – will become greater if the thought is not merely a casual notice of the idea, but is close, full and prolonged attention. Close, full and prolonged attention in thought is what is called meditation. It is the opposite of going to sleep. And just as increased pressure of thought upon the idea of the cow increases the knowledge of the cow, so it also should increase the knowledge of the thought – just as the pressure of the foot on the ground increases the knowledge about the ground *and* the knowledge about the foot, that is, improves the contact *both ways*, so in meditation both the object and the thinking quality are improved.

Now we come to the nub of the question. There is a third element in this situation – 'I'. There are I and the thought on one occasion; there are I and the object on another occasion. The first of these is a meditative occasion. There can be a new kind of meditation, which is the pressure of the I upon the thought which gives stronger contact with it, greater awareness of thinking. It also gives greater awareness of 'I'. So, *while the thinking is going on* you must give attention to the 'I', so as to experience 'being I' to the full. You will then know the self-nature as well as the other-nature. You cannot know the foot if you abolish the ground. You cannot know the self if you abolish the thought. But this knowing of self is not sense-knowing (ground-knowing) and it is not thought-knowing (idea-knowing). But at the time of self-knowing you are not reft away from the self-knowing, by importunate desires of ground-knowing or of idea-knowing.

It is because of this that our contact with Nature enriches us so much. What the birds in the garden have in their bodily life which I have not in my bodily life becomes mine because I come to know what it is like to be what they are. This is where Zen attentiveness to Nature is important. The foot feels the foot when it feels the ground.

Nembutsu. Reverence to Buddha. (See under Pure Land Sect.)

Niao-ka. A famous Zen Master, who quoted the following poem on the occasion of a visit from the Governor of the province:

> Not to commit evils,
> But to practice all good,
> And to keep the heart pure –
> This is the teaching of the Buddhas.

It was the habit of this Master to sit on a platform which he had built up in a tree. The Governor remarked that that was rather a precarious position, but the Master replied that it was not as dangerous as the Governor's, for he was constantly under the danger of passionateness and mental strain.

Nichiren. A patriotic enthusiast who established a sect based upon the Tendai School of Mahāyāna Buddhism, but selecting the last fourteen chapters of the *Lotus Sutra* as the essential doctrine of 'the original Buddha'. In those chapters Buddha spoke of his original being, as distinguished from his incarnation. Nichiren wanted the other Sects to be suppressed by the Government, and denounced them in strong terms: 'Jodo sect is hell, Zen is devil, Shingon will cause national collapse, and Ritzu is an enemy of the country!'

Nidānas. The chain of twelve causes in the course of a lifetime, taught by Buddha and recorded in the Mahāvagga. This is not concerned with Zen as such, but is a statement of the course of life generally accepted by Buddhists. The entire cycle of a human life is thus: (1) ignorance (avidyā), which is the awakening of the whole process, (2) the activation of the habit-moulds (sanskāras or sankhāras) in the three worlds (*q.v.*), (3) recognition of objects (vijnana or vinnāna), (4) the setting up of names and forms (nāmarūpa), (5) the awakening of the six organs of sense (shadāyatana), (6) contact with things (sparsha or phassa), (7) feelings of pleasure or pain therefrom (vedana), (8) desire to enjoy or to avoid (trishnā or tanhā), (9) attachment and activity (upadāna), (10) coming to birth (bhāva), (11) condition and class of the body (jāti), and (12) the series of old age (jarā), death (marana), grief (shoka), lamentation (paridevana), pain (dukkha) and dejection or mental affliction (durmanas). These are particularly referred to by Huang Po (Obaku) in the Wan Ling record written down by P'ei Hsin.

It will be noticed that the nidānas from (2) to (9) refer to life in the womb, before the birth of the body.

Nirmānakāya. The 'manifestation body' or 'incarnation body' of Buddha or a buddha. (See also Kāyas.)

Nirvāna. Perhaps the clearest introductory statement in our language anent Nirvāna is that given in two verses of Edwin Arnold's *Light of Asia*, as follows:

> If any teach Nirvāna is to cease,
>   Say unto such they lie.
> If any teach Nirvāna is to live,
>   Say unto such they err; not knowing this,
> Nor what light shines beyond their broken lamps,
>   Nor lifeless, timeless, bliss.

The word Nirvāna means literally a blowing-out, as in the extinguishing of a candle flame. It thus has a negative form, following upon the fulfilment of the Four Noble Truths – (1) The fact of sorrow; (2) Sorrow's cause – desire; (3) The ceasing of sorrow – by the conquest of desire, and (4) The Noble Eightfold Path – or way of life for the ceasing of sorrow. However, both the Path and its goal (Nirvāna) are referred to as more joy-giving than the life of perpetual creation of new sorrows by the operation of personal desire. Here is the statement about the Path:

> Enter the path! There is no grief like Hate!
>   No pains like passion, no deceit like sense!
> Enter the path! far hath he gone whose foot
>   Treads down one fond offence.
> Enter the path! There spring the healing streams
>   Quenching all thirst! there bloom th' immortal flowers
> Carpeting all the way with joy! there throng
>   Swiftest and sweetest hours!

And there is also the personal testimony of Buddha:

> I, Buddh, who wept with all my brothers' tears,
>   Whose heart was broken by a whole world's woe,
> Laugh and am glad, for there is Liberty!
>   Ho! Ye who suffer! know
> Ye suffer from yourself.
>   None else compels . . .

It is clear from these quotations that although Buddha would not approve of any positive description of Nirvāna, he did so because it has no qualities conceivable by the mind – no comparison with anything thinkable or presented in the form of matter, and he was declaring a *positive* and joyous knowledge. Indeed the title 'Buddha' arose from that – as it derives from the verbal root budh, to know. There was no negativity about it, except the denial that it could be thought about, or known by or through the senses.

To the Zenist, this shows the main aim of dhyāna or meditation. These are the people who put it first in the religious programme – whose motto is, so to say, 'Do it now.' With them it is not a case of seeking pleasure, however refined, however 'heavenly'. Only if 'heaven' is 'Taoic' or 'Nirvānic', will they have any dealing with that term. They hold that it is within us and all about us, but not known by us if our attention is wholly occupied with mind and sense. Nor is it known by any sort of 'I and it', or 'I and you' relation. Some have said it is known only by a kind of direct perception entirely devoid of the subject and object relation.

Whether the nirvāna-realization is the same as satori (q.v.) depends upon the definition of satori. If satori is 'intuition' it is not the same, for intuitions are often of the mind and have degrees accordingly.

But if the satori is of the 'Buddha-mind', not of the human mind, then it may well be the same, since Buddha-mind is 'what Buddha knew', and that is the full fruit of Satori.

rvāna Sūtra. A scripture which emphasizes the importance of Buddha-nature, which is the same as self-nature.

-mind (wu-hsin). Bodhidharma brought with him to China the Indian view that all this world comes from mind – what we may call Divine Mind, since it is beyond all limitations, just as the sun is beyond all clouds. His successors in office up to the Fifth Patriarch held diverse views under this general idea, but all agreed that meditation should be such as to favour the reception of this pure light without stain or dust. The monk's mind was to be 'a mirror bright' and must not 'gather dust while it reflects', which means that he must be on guard. It was only upon the insight and statement of the Sixth Patriarch, Hui-neng, who was at the time a working monk in the monastery, that the doctrine of 'no-mind' came forward. (See under Hui-neng, mirror, etc.) In the meditation of his predecessors the process was one of duality, looking at the pure mind and receiving its light, but Hui-neng insisted that the meditation should be pure seeing, and such pure seeing alone would give the truth. It was not looking at the reality, but looking as it, and only so could the truth or essence of things be realized.

It is interesting to note that a very similar method was given by Patanjali centuries earlier, when he defined samādhi in his Sutra III 3, as dhyāna in which there is the shining of the mere objects above, as if devoid (Shūnya) of one's own form. This is looking without self, without bias, without a point of view. Hui-neng's term was Chien-hsing, translated as 'to look into the true nature', while the term used before his time was k'an-ching, which implies watching an object as a spectator from the outside. He maintained that even the notion of aiming at the purity of the true Mind was to ascribe to it an erroneous limitation, so the monk in his meditation must be completely empty of expectation or desire. He is to have no idea about the satori, and will not be able to describe it in any mental terms even when he has realized it. So Hui-neng demanded shūnyatā (emptiness), the avoidance of all qualities as prerequisite to true seeing, and so no mind qualities, or better, no-mind, in the dhyāna. He was equally against the thought of being quiet or passive. Notions of purity, of quietness, of emptiness, are all notions which bind back. If there is the notion of seeing into one's own self-nature, it must be entertained only without any definitions. Hence Hui-neng's formula: 'From the first not a thing is.' There is something similar in the Vedanta philosopher's 'neti, neti,' – not thus, not thus – used in the search for the infinite, in which (as explained in my *Glorious*

Presence) one must 'not' also the not, but there is perhaps this difference, that in Hui-neng the seeing is all and in the Vedanta the seen is all. In both cases, however, subject and object are both transcended.

Non-action. See under Wu-wei.

Number. This is sometimes referred to in connection with the Avatanshaka Sutra (*q.v.*), where it teaches that there is no number, 'neither one nor two'. The idea is that once we enter in thought into the region beyond duality, that is, into the 'Buddha-mind', multiplicity disappears, but so does unity, if we mean one-ness by that word. In brief, we have reached beyond classification, including numbers. (See also under One-ness.)

Nyoi. A fancy stick, made of various materials, sometimes carried by Zen monks. It has been thought to symbolize and remind one of the mixed-up contents of one's ordinary unpurified mind.

baku. In Chinese, Huang Po (*q.v.*).

baku Sect, The. Founded by the Chinese philosopher, Huang Po (Obaku) in the seventeenth century, and later included in the Rinzai Sect. The Obaku Sect of Zen has more than 550 temples.

ne-ness. As no one knows the universe as 'one' reality, the term 'unity' is better, for we do see the unity or non-separateness, and indeed interdependence, of all the things we know.

Not a grain of dust can get away and exist separately or alone. The term 'one' can be very misleading, because one is only a number like any other number. From the standpoint of a half, one is a two, etc. Two, etc., are also units, as two spoons, e.g., are 'a two' of spoons. There is thus no uniqueness in the number one, which originated from our (illusory) perception of 'separate objects'. So the absolute is not to be designated by any number, not even 'one'. Therefore also nirvāna cannot be designated as the one in contrast with the manifest universe as the many.

It is considered that the old Chinese Zen Masters – who were already familiar with the principle of Tao – saw everything in nature as interrelated with everything else, and so did not regard some as good and others as bad, or some as superior or higher and others as inferior or lower. This is quite in agreement with modern science also, by which we can say that everything is what it is and where it is because of everything else – and itself.

P

Pai-chang Nich-p'an. Hyakujyo (*q.v.*).

Paramārtha (499–569). Noted translator of Buddhist scriptures into Chinese, particularly the highly prized Surangama Sūtra (*q.v.*).

Pāramitās. Perfections, of which there are six, namely: (1) Dāna: giving; charity and love. (2) Shīla: harmony; good conduct; morality. (3) Kshānti: patience, that nought can ruffle. (4) Vīrya: valour; bravery; vigour. (5) Dhyāna: contemplation; meditation. (6) Prajnā: (*q.v.*).

The first five of these are not to be confused with Perfection, or the great perfection (mahā-pāramitā), which is Prajnā-pāramitā. One may imagine a perfect circle, or a perfect dog or a perfect man. Still, these are not 'perfection'. The first five in the list are perfections of mind, including heart and will. The mature or perfect *mind* will have these five, and is then ready for the great adventure. Arhat, though a term not commonly used by Zenists, means ready for, worthy of, or deserving of the perfection beyond human perfection.

Patriarchs, Indian. When Buddha gave his 'transmission without words' to Mahākāshyapa, he thereby became the first Indian Patriarch of what is now called Zen. Afterwards Mahākāshyapa made the same transmission to the disciple Ananda, who thus became second Indian Patriarch. The series continued until Bodhidharma (*q.v.*), who was the twenty-eighth.

The names of the third to the twenty-seventh were, in order, Shānakavāsa, Upagupta, Dhritaka, Michchhaka, Vasumitra, Buddhanandi, Buddhamitra, Pārshwa, Punyayashas, Ashwaghosha, Kapimala, Nāgārjuna, Kānadeva, Rāhulata, Sanghānandi, Gayashāta, Kumarāta, Jayata, Vasubandhu, Manorhita, Haklena, Āryasinha, Basyasita, Punyamitra and Prajnātāra.

This is the generally accepted list, as arranged by a monk named K'i-sung (11th century), based upon information in the *Fa-fa-t'sang-chuan*, used by the Tien-tai (Tendai) School.

Patriarchs, Zen. The six Zen Patriarchs of China were: (1) Bodhidharma, (2) Hui-ke, (3) Seng-tsan, (4) Tao-hsin, (5) Hung-jen, and (6) Shen-shiu (according to the Northern School) or Hui-neng (according to the Southern School). The Japanese names of these Patriarchs are (1) Daruma, (2) Yeka or Eka, (3) Sisan, (4) Doshin, (5) Gunin, and (6) Yeno or Eno (i.e., for Hui-neng). Bodhidharma, who came from India, is listed as the twenty-eighth Zen Patriarch of that country.

eace. The peace of mind attained in Zen is not of the strenuous or courageous variety. An outstanding example of it occurred when Kaisen Osho, a famous general in the Japanese civil wars, was burnt to death. He left the following verse:

> For quiet sitting in meditation
> No need for a place by a mountain stream;
> When the mind is entirely extinguished
> Even the fire is cool and refreshing.

ersecution, The Great. There was a great persecution of the Buddhists in China in the last century of the T'ang Dynasty (A.D. 618–907), especially under the Emperor Wu-tsung in A.D. 845, which destroyed 4600 monasteries and caused a quarter of a million monks and nuns to return to ordinary life.

The decline of Buddhism in China at that time was therefore very great, except in the School of Zen, which soon recovered what little ground it may have lost. Indeed, not long afterwards, in the Sung period, it reached its greatest popularity and height. With the advancement in popularity and the building of many grand Zen monasteries, there was an influx of disciples. Then, as quantity increased, quality decreased, and there came about a reduction in the earnestness of the seeking of the Buddha-mind, at which in the earlier period the movement had been exclusively aimed. There was also a tendency towards mingling with other sects, which led to intellectual interests, not wanted in Zen practice.

The great Hui-neng had died in 713, but his followers established five well-known Zen schools ('houses' – goke, in Japanese), namely the Ikyo or Igyo, the Rinzai, the Ummon, the Soto and the Hogen. It was at this point that a separation occurred, the distinction between Tathāgata Zen and Patriarchal Zen became prominent, and the latter became dominant in the Zen movement in the form of Kanna Zen, especially in the Rinzai school. Three of the five Zen 'houses' died away in China in the Sung period and only the Rinzai and the Soto remained, and still remain, the Rinzai being far larger and stronger than the Soto. Later, in Japan, the Soto became much larger than the Rinzai.

oetry. See under Haiku and Arts of Zen.

o-yin. Hakuin (*q.v.*).

rajnā. Essential wisdom, as distinguished from either Sanjñā or Vijñā, awareness of objects or environment and their use and value. Some have translated prajñā as 'transcendent wisdom', which means that i transcends the knowledge of things, and also of the mind. This means that prajñā is knowing or consciousness or awareness as such, beyond the duality of subject and object, but not transcendent in the sense o knowledge of a *state* or region outside or beyond the world of operation which is ordinary life. To assume 'another world' with which one attains contact on reaching illumination is contrary to the spiri of Zen. To call it a 'state' would be the attribution to it of a menta conception, thereby denying its beyond-mindness or 'no-mind' knowing. In Zen, prajñā is equated to Buddha-mind, because it is taken to name Buddha's illumination, and also equated to the void – void o the limitations of body and mind. It is knowing knowing knowing (i.e. subject, predicate and object all being the same).

Just as animals, it is presumed, have mind without knowing or saying to themselves, 'I have mind,' so do most human beings have consciousness (prajñā) without knowing it as such. The mind cannot know it.

The word prajñā is composed of two parts – pra and jna. Jna is a Sanskrit verbal root meaning to know, and pra means 'going forth' (pro in many English words). So the knight is now standing ready in his armour and fully equipped. Then comes the sanjñā. The prefix san means togetherness, which implies at least a duality. So sanjñā is knowledge with duality, i.e. knowledge *of* something. The knight has now joined issue with an enemy.

This distinction between prajñā and sanjñā is worthy of careful attention. Much confusion has arisen because in Buddha's teaching of the twelve nidānas (successive causes), he gives vijñāna as the third item in a list of the successive occurrences of a lifetime, and this has sometimes been translated simply 'consciousness', instead of 'consciousness-of' implying an external something. First on the list of causes comes ignorance, second comes the revival of residues and tendencies from the past (sanskāras), third the vijñā, and so on. (See under Nidānas.) Prajñā is, of course, prior to and behind the whole list. In this matter, and in all matters, the Zenist is careful not to confuse prajñā with vijñā or sanjñā, or with anything else.

Turning for a moment to the Hindu scriptures, we find prajñā used in the sense of the wisdom, or insight, of one who (so to speak) has his eye on the 'owner of the body' all the time, amidst all the affairs of life. This is in the *Bhagavad Gitā*, where it is the theme of the teaching in Chapter 2. Again, it appears in the *Dhammapada*, a very famous Theravada scripture, where Buddha says, in the chapter on The Bhikku (monk), verse 13; that without prajñā there is no (real) meditation, and without meditation there is no prajñā.

This is, one thinks, the most important word in all the vocabulary of Zen. It contains or implies illumination (sambodhi), the Beyond (para or nirvāna), the Void (shūnyatā), Buddha-nature, all-knowledge. It is indeed perfection (pāramitā). Before illumination, therefore, and to keep the ordinary mind (chitta) in line, Zenists often permit themselves to *worship* the Prajnā-pāramitā, and treat with reverence the very book or scripture which deals with it, with all the materials and forms of adoration, such as altars, garlands, incense, lamps, flags, robes, and prostrations. Thus the energizing effect of emotion is also kept in tune with the deepest understanding.

Prajnā-Pāramitā Sūtra. A very old Mahāyāna scripture, or rather collection of scriptures. Various parts of it were translated into Chinese by Kumārajīva and others. The first to be published had 8000 verses, but the whole is believed to amount to more than 125,000. The work is very repetitious, but this is usually considered quite desirable in the East, where students like to go over the same ideas again and again, as their habit of pondering often leads to intuition. The portion called Vajra-chchhedika (diamond cutter) which deals especially with ohūnyatā (emptiness), first appeared in English in a translation by Max Muller and William Geurmel. The overall purpose of all of it is connected with the aim of the Bodhisattwa, with very much attention to Prajnā, the sixth of the perfections (pāramitās, *q.v.*), treated by no means as an abstraction, but as including both the absolute and the relative.

Pranidhāna. Often called a vow, but more exactly a dedication. An analysis of the components of the word gives a very accurate idea of it. These are pra, ni and dha, equal to forth, under and placing. The word is much used in Mahāyāna Buddhism in reference to the dedication of the Bodhisattwa and the aspirant to Bodhisattwahood, in which he affirms that he will not accept nirvāna, or at least will not leave the sansāra until all are ready for the same freedom. The going forth part of it involves the karuna, which is, so to say, the love side of the realization of the unity involved in the idea of nirvāna.

In that compassion the Bodhisattwa very naturally mingles with others and does not retreat into solitude. Further, this mingling as shown in the Prajnā-pāramitā Sūtra is not in any patronizing or superior mood, but as one of them. If it does not involve the same mental suffering it is because of the prajnā which accompanies it, that is, the wisdom which in the midst of living sees the value of living, and the supreme importance of limitations, none of which are trifles, but even the most trifling of which contains the supremely important truth that for the awakening of self-realization the most trifling thing is as potent as the greatest.

The comparison of method of the Bodhisattwa and that of the Shrāvaka (hearer), who studies the scriptures, entirely intent upon

Prajnā, or ultimate knowledge of that by which all things are understood (as one of the Upanishads has it) – presents us with a picture
of the fact that wisdom is love as well as knowledge, which are two
forms of the experience of unity, one in the feelings and the other in
the thinkings. While each has its appropriate mode of life, the fulfilment of either must be the fulfilment of both.

The consistent Zenist usually appears to be one who, while intent
upon truth, can in some measure penetrate to the perception of the
principle of all-satisfying unity in the external particulars in nature,
as well as in what is (in reality) also an external particular which he
calls 'myself'.

In both cases the joy of the goal throws its light to some extent upon
the way thereto, so that the aspirant experiences a constant glow, and
occasionally a brilliant unexpected light. The two paths converge as
they approach the goal, so that the often maligned Pratyeka-Buddha,
one who finds nirvāna for himself alone, turns out to be only an
imaginary 'whipping-boy'.

Prince and Minister. See under Soto.

Pure Land Sect. In Chinese, Ching-t'u; in Japanese, Jodo; the respective
founders being Hui-yuan and Honen who lived 334–416 and 1133–
1212. This, the most popular form of Buddhism in Japan, is not
entirely zenic. It differs from Zen in that it allows for salvation
through others, not by one's own merit alone. (See under Tāriki.)
Particularly, there is the practice of nembutsu, which is the daily
repetition of 'Namo Amitābha' ('Namu-Amida-Butsu', in Japanese).
This is accompanied by a belief in salvation for all through trust in
Amida (Buddha), because the Buddha-nature is present in all, and
because in fact all and each are indissolubly together always.

In addition to the nembutsu there is the recitation of vows listed
in a text named *Sukhāvatī Vyūha*. It is from this word Sukhāvatī,
which means 'having happiness', referring to a region or heavenly
state after death, that the belief in the Pure Land arose. The text
promises birth in this land as the effect of the nembutsu. In this state,
also called the 'Western Paradise of Bliss', the devotees are taught
by Avalokiteshwara how to achieve Buddhahood, so that the entire
method is called the Easy Way, as contrasted with the Hard Way of
Zen and other methods. There is philosophy in the idea of this attainment, on the ground that the Buddha-nature is, after all, present in
all, and so you are invoking your own true self.

Buddha stated in the *Shanmun-yi-Tung*, that some of the residents
of this happy region or state are temporary and will return to future
births on earth, while others are 'avaivartya', which means not
coming and going but permanent residents. The same text calls it also
'the holy abode of arhats', indicating the idea that arhats need not

return to birth on earth unless they wish to do so. Sukhāvatī is regarded as a place or condition after death in which the meditation or devotion is carried on effectively, conducing to a favourable advance towards illumination by the kindness of Amida, whether in the individual case there be a return to birth after some time, or not.

There are four Sects of Jodo in Japan, with minor differences: Jodo proper, with about four million followers; Shin, with about thirteen million; Yuzunembutsu and Ji, much smaller, with only a few thousands each.

R

Reality. Spoken of as the unattainable. Yet as all things have reality, they can be known with prajñā. The conception of reality as including both being and non-being together may be reached by regarding it as the summum genus. Everywhere there are things and also absences or nothings, in various ways, such as the 'present absence' or 'nothing' of, say, Julius Caesar. This is present absence. There is the future absence of our bodies after death and destruction. There was the 'past absence' of the bird while still an egg. So in the totality of things there are presences of things and absences of things, and there is the nothing which is space. Both something and nothing (thing and space or absence) are real. So reality is in both, though each of them is less than reality.

Reason or Nature. This is a serious consideration for Zenists, indeed for all who hold that the human race must 'carve out' its own future – a fact which is virtually accepted by all rationalists, and has been well presented to the world by Dr Julian Huxley in his *Religion Without Revelation*. It will probably be generally accepted before long that this is essentially a dynamic world or – in other words – all things are what they *do*, not what they *are*. This world is – as old India held – a world of *action*, even to the extent that Buddha carried the view when he declared that man *is* action, not a continuing *self*, but a changing integrate. (See under Anatta Doctrine.)

To understand this, a very strong and clear distinction must be made between integration and aggregation. In the theory of evolution it is the 'coherence' factor, not the 'aggregation' (whether homogeneous or heterogeneous) factor, which is the prime cause of form and action. The word 'coherence' also needs consideration; it is inherent coherence that is seen in evolution, not adherent coherence. A bus may contain fifty people going from one town to another. Those people are an aggregate unit, not an integrate unity. In contrast with this we may inspect an animal body, with its miscellaneous organs and limbs all serving one another; here we have an integrate unity, not an aggregate unit.

Now, what an integrate does is an action, what an aggregate does is not an action, but merely a motion. A banner flapping in the wind moves, but it does not act. This being the case how does a man act? If we were considering only a man's hand and asking 'How does it (now) act?' we might say, 'By holding' or 'By letting go', or 'With a pen'. Similarly, we may say of a man that he thinks or reasons, 'Shall I pick up the hammer or the pen?' 'Why', 'which' and 'how' all come into his actions – all brought in by reason.

The *action of the mind* which has been called reasoning has proved very useful in the business of integration, both for the preservation of a man and for his acts of aggregation, or relation to others and to things, that is, for his actions in relation to his environment. Reason is useful in relation to outside things, and even to the body itself, to affirm and preserve its organic integrity, and its power of action in its environment. But reason itself grows stronger, in both its grip and its grasp – that is, in its power and its extent – while it is being used. The man's actions thus grow stronger and greater in relation to his environment, either by conquest or by adaptation. We have reached the point in human evolution where actions of adaptations have almost ceased – the body now hardly changes its form – and actions of conquest have taken over. The mind has come into power.

It may be remarked that reason also must be regarded as natural. Yes, and as reason is always concerned with action – action to preserve or action to change – it must be regarded as a definite factor in nature, on the side of law and order. But the Zenist seeks a deeper fact – beyond doing, in being.

eincarnation. The belief that living beings, including man, have a series of bodily lives, only ceasing when they no longer base their happiness on any of the objects of the world. This comes about when the Buddha-nature is found. This belief is common to all Buddhists. The idea is that if you do not reach the goal, or 'the other shore' in this incarnation, you have always another chance. In one school at least it is held that having reached this end, the pilgrim is asekha (one who has more to learn), but this is not a matter of accumulation of knowledge, but of appreciation of the true nature of everything one meets with, and thus realization of their unity in or as the One Reality.

Sometimes the original word for reincarnation (punarjanman – literally, again-birth) is translated as transmigration, which is conventionally taken to mean that a man may be reborn as an animal if his addiction to some animal propensity is strong enough, as his desires and actions (karma) carry him into the conditions in which they can be gratified, but some hold that the popular stories about men becoming pigs, tigers, wolves, vultures and even worms are allegorical, and really mean pig-like men, etc., since there are plenty of such to be seen in human bodies. However, in all cases it is regarded as education, not punishment.

It is the same doctrine of rebirth as was rejected from the Christian Church at the Council of Alexandria in A.D. 550, at which one third of the Bishops voted for the doctrine, and two thirds against it.

Rinzai, Enlightenment of. The story of Rinzai's enlightenment is as follows. When he had been for three years in the Obaku school he approached the Master personally and asked what was the essential truth in Buddha's teaching: all he got was twenty blows with a stick. He went to another Master, Daigu (Ta-yu), who told him that Obaku had given him the correct treatment for his enlightenment, and further emphasized the matter by roughly manhandling Rinzai's throat and subjecting him to harsh words. This time Rinzai hit back, striking Daigu in the ribs. Nevertheless, he had suddenly become enlightened.

Next, Rinzai went back to Obaku to tell him what had happened, but the Master only threatened him with more and gave him a slap in the face, whereupon Obaku gave way to great laughter and roared out the meaningless shout 'Katsu'.

If such treatments are intended to stop the student from dreaming along or from resorting to explanations which are fundamentally only comparisons (what a Vedantist would call ascriptions – adhyāsa) and direct him back from words to direct experience, well and good if the teacher administers his 'teaching' at the right moment. All the same, other Masters have favoured gentle methods. Of this nature was the teaching of a mother to her little son – a modern case. The boy had been pulling legs off spiders and watching their reflex movements with considerable intellectual interest. Wishing to enhance this enjoyment, he ran to his mother and demonstrated the phenomenon before her. 'Look, mother,' he urged. The mother exclaimed, 'Don't, don't, you are hurting the spider!' Whether from the mother's words or from some manner or tone or gesture of hers, the occasion proved appropriate, for the little boy suddenly 'realized' that the spider was a living being. One is tempted to add 'like himself', but those words are too explanatory. It was a direct experience, of permanent value.

In modern America the attraction to Zen today is definitely of the Rinzai type, but rather much as children watch on television the scalping and other exploits of some of the Red Indians of the past. When they afterwards think of this portion of their memories' contents, they see the value of direct experience in the evolution or awakening of man. The recounting and review of the Rinzai beatings and shoutings call up no emulation in the respectable audiences at the public lectures on Zen, but they do drive home the lesson of direct experience *versus* inference about the Buddha-mind.

Rinzai Gigen (d.867). Also known as Lin-chi. Founder of the Rinzai Sect of Zen. (See also under Sudden School, and Rinzai's Enlightenment.)

Rinzairoku. A book containing the sayings and sermons of Rinzai, the founder of the Rinzai Sect. (See also under Sesshin.)

Roshi. The title of a Zen Master. When a disciple or pupil, whether monk or lay student, has completed his studies, and his master has been satisfied that the pupil's understanding is equal to his own, and that the student has experienced genuine satori, he may bestow the title of Roshi upon him. This entitles him to teach Zen. In the Rinzai schools a course in the study of koans is given, and only those who have been through this are entitled to offer instruction in koans.

Rūpa and Arūpa. These two adjectives are usually taken as meaning 'having form' and 'without form', respectively. But there is a correction required to this thought, since the prefix a- is not merely a negative but a contrast. Thus, if jnāna means knowledge ajnāna means error, not mere absence of knowledge.

When, therefore, 'manas' (thought), or 'buddhi' (understanding) is called arūpa it does not mean that they are nothing in themselves, but that they exist in a state which is not that of form – they have no length, breadth and thickness, have no extensity, do not occupy space, yet are just as real as the other category.

An old question in Europe was: 'How many angels can dance on the point of a needle?' And the answer is: 'An infinite number of angels can dance on the point of a needle.' But how can we see it? When you release yourself from the domination of your space-impulse.

It has been said that when a sculptor makes a statue by chipping away the unwanted part of the stone, he does not 'make the form' but releases the form which was there all the time. Really, he has bound the form, and imprisoned it, separated it from its 'friends', namely, all the other forms which were also in that block of stone.

Ryokan. Zen poet. (See under Stories.)

S

Saddharma-pundarīka. Literally, 'The lotus of the True Law'. This scripture has a great vogue in China and Japan, especially in the Tien-tai (Tendai) and Nichiren sects. It was first translated into Chinese as far back as about A.D. 250. A later translation by Kumāra-jīva is used all over China and Japan, along with commentaries by Chih-i. The Lotus Sūtra teaches, among other things, that the truth can be indicated by means other than words, such as gestures and exclamations and silences.

Saijo Zen. The last stage in the practice of za-zen, in which there is a complete absence of striving. This condition involves (1) harikitte, alertness of reaching out, like a taut bowstring, (2) nombiri, unhurried and relaxed from all tension or haste, (3) dosshiri, steadiness, like Mount Fuji or a great rock, (4) rinzen, complete withdrawal from all distractions of the senses. It is the continuation of Mahāyāna meditation or daijozen after satori has been to some extent experienced.

In this there is no aim or purpose, but 'just sitting' in the right mood (sometimes called shikan-tanza) so as to allow satori to fulfil itself. It is far removed from mere idle sitting. It illustrates the fact that 'meditation is the opposite to going to sleep'. In the Indian system this truth is brought strongly to light by the statement that meditation begins with an act of concentration, in which the conscious awareness reaches its greatest clarity and strength, and that clarity and strength are then carried further on into the meditation. This is really strenuous, but is quite compatible with non-tension in the body and tranquillity in the mind.

Samādhi. An activity of the mind, poising itself upon an object or idea, especially when the mind has already fully worked upon the object or idea, and has come to a dead end or a paradox. It differs from concentration in that concentration is the mere focusing of attention on a 'ground' (object or idea). A samādhi has been preceded by a flow of thought concerning that ground. Patanjali has well described the distinction of concentration, meditation and contemplation (samādhi) in his Yoga Sūtras III, 1–11.

Sambhogakāya. The enjoyment or conscious or super-mind 'body' or state of a Buddha. (See under Kāyas.)

Samurai. The warrior class of Japan, much influenced by Zen. (See under Bushido and Arts of Zen.)

Sangha. An assembly or brotherhood of monks. The Buddhist monastic order. Satsang means 'good company' or 'beneficial companionship' of several or many persons, or association with the good.

Sansāra. The round of births and deaths. The region 'outside nirvāna'. The 'wheel of life'.

San-zen. A private interview between Zen Master and pupil. In the Rinzai school koans and mondos may then be used. (See under Koan-Interview.)

Satori. Illumination or enlightenment. In Zen, the state of consciousness of the Buddha-mind. Consciousness of pure consciousness itself, as such, without objects either mental or bodily. Prajnā.

If the experience can be characterized either mentally or emotionally it is not *the* satori, although the word is sometimes used loosely to indicate great mental or emotional heightening and flooding, of the nature of intuition. In the Zenist schools it definitely means seeing into one's own essential nature, and finding something quite new which is known with great clarity and illumines the whole of life, but cannot be expressed in any way.

At the same time it must be said that an intuition may indicate the inner experience of satori, which for an instant has cast its illumination into the mind, but is lost sight of in the process of being noticed. In the sage's satori, however, the satori casts its influence in exactly that way but is not lost in the process.

The Zenist does not wait for satori to come to him, but has his own special mode of meditation leading to it. (See also under Wu-wei, and Anuttara-samyak-sambodhi.)

Sayings of Zen Masters. There are several large collections of these – namely, *The Transmission of the Lamp*, *The Five Lamps meeting at the Source*, *The Finger Pointing at the Moon*, and *The Imperial Selection of Chan Sayings*, from the last of which the *Mumonkan* (*q.v.*) is a selection. Many of these sayings are given in Lu Kuan Yu's two recent volumes entitled *Ch'an and Zen Teaching*.

Seer and Seen. In pure seeing this duality disappears. The disappearance of this duality is the moment of realization, because all seeing is uniting in some degree. It begins in interest, or mental desire. Without interest a simple creature would not turn from one thing to another – food, etc. And once interest is aroused, there is the desire 'to be with' or 'to have', which is an impulse to union, and to fulfilment.

91

When seeing is complete, there is the rapture or samādhi or satori of non-duality – no 'I and thou' but the enjoyment of the total or united be-ing. It is rather the seen that is absorbed into the seer, than the seer being absorbed by the seen, so the essential self (the Buddha-mind) remains. The zenic assertion with regard to this is that it can be a matter of will, when will replaces wishes. This is the result of meditation on the mind, which leads to perception of the undesirability of wishing. When wishing goes, antagonism goes and there is the experience of the completeness of the unity of seer and seen, which is also freedom, because as the Stoics used to put it, 'Nothing happens contrary to my will.'

A philosophic aspect of this is the idea that everything is my superior in that it has something which I have not. A peaceful union with that other is therefore very fulfilling. 'The discarding of dualism' is therefore 'the womb of Tathāgata'. This was also propounded by the Indian sage Shankarāchārya, when he gave a full meaning to the yogic practice of yama (restraint) by saying, in his book *Aparokshā-nubhūti* (Direct Experience):

'Restraint (yama) is that poise of the village of sensations which arises from the knowledge that everything is Brahman; it should be practised again and again.' (Translation by Ernest Wood, in *The Glorious Presence*.)

The Zenists maintain that everything that occurs is worthy of our most appreciative attention. There is no need to seek somewhere else for what is worthwhile. Poise means that we stop the mental running about which goes on constantly like a panic. But if we believe that what is contained in the present experience of drinking, let us say, a cup of tea, is supremely valuable, there will be a release from mental feverishness. It will be an experience in itself, not a preparation for some other experience. This is not a mere relaxation of mind. It is a perfection of mind. This poise can be present with all the successive activities of body and mind at all times. It awaits us but we cannot seek it. It is the true life in relation to experience. It is Zen.

Seigen Gyoshi. Hsing Szu, in Chinese. The follower of Hui-neng who spread the movement southward from Horin.

Sekito Kisen. In Chinese, Shih Tou. Follower and successor of Seigen Gyoshi, who lived in a hut built by himself. His doctrine of the unity of the absolute and the relative, and 'light' with 'darkness', in his *Sandokai*, led to the later 'five ranks' of the Soto Zenists. (See under Circles and Soto.) After Sekito the Seigen school divided; one line, through Yakusan Igen, leading on to the formation of the Soto Sect, the other giving rise to the Ummon and Hogen Schools.

Self. What you are you are, and you are unique in nature and in Nature. This applies to all things. A piece of stone here appears to be similar to a piece of stone over there – same shape, size, colour and composition. But it is here and that is there. Cow in the barn is not the same as cow in the field. It reflects into others and others reflect into it, and each with its own ultimate uniqueness. You are what your response is, but that response is what it is because of your own uniqueness and the uniqueness of the circumstances. So you are not absolutely you and the circumstances are not absolutely circumstances. This being so, your attempt to see yourself as only part of yourself – namely, a thing of thoughts and feelings and actions – is bound to lead to a piece of false knowing, lessening the fullness of life, and not permitting the response of the whole self to its whole environment. And yet, do what you will, even this non-response is natural to you, so there is no completely natural response of whole man to whole environment.

There is also always the future and the past as well as the here and the there. That 'future in the present' is adaptation, and thought is adaptation of a particular part of oneself to a particular part of the environment; and such adaptiveness is part of our present uniqueness, as much as legs or eyes. So here we are back at the beginning but with thought and planning, though not with self-definition.

So the answer to 'What are you?' is 'I am what *I* am,' and to 'What do you mean by that statement?' is 'What I mean.' 'What is the significance of five inches?' 'That it is five inches, now, but for adaptation it can be used.' It is not five times one inch, nor ten times half an inch, nor any collection of such statements. Every number is unique. Everything is unique.

It has been made clear by Zen teachings, however, that one never loses one's true Self even amidst the errors and delusions, or rather illusions, and also that one does not gain it at the time of enlightenment, since it was always there.

Self-nature, Seeing into one's. In Chinese, tzu-hsing. It is taken for granted that one's own nature is not the same as that of anything known to the mind. Therefore it cannot be expressed in any terms known to the mind. Otherwise one would be somewhat in the position of a certain inmate in a mental home who was quite sane on all points except that of his own identity. The story goes that he had shown a visitor round the institution and explained everything very well, but suddenly, as the guest was about to leave, he struck an attitude, with one hand on hip and the other held up and outwards, and said, 'Pour me out, please; I'm a teapot.'

Self-knowing cannot even be seeing in the sense of one thing seeing another. As explained by the Indian Vedantist Shankarāchārya in his *Drig-drishya-Viveka*, the seen cannot be the seer. That being the case, it is no wonder that in becoming aware of one's own nature the

Zenists have been forced into a paradoxical expression – the seeing that is no seeing.

It is, of course, well known that some creatures, for example, very young babies, are very conscient and sentient before the awakening of mental operations which distinguish definite objects in the environment. They are conscious of self without any thought or definition of self. That knowledge is ours throughout life. To characterize that knowing as in any way the knowing of an object is to make the error known as adhyāsa, defined as the ascription to a thing of some quality or character previously seen elsewhere. This is what the mind does when it demands a definition of something in terms of its points of resemblance to and difference from something else. Such occurs when, for example, a child first hears of a tiger and asks what it is, and is told, 'Well, it is like a cat, but is larger, etc., etc.' So with regard to the self, its nature is such that it (strictly one should not even say 'it') cannot be in the category of anything seen. So even the looking at it is 'no-looking', and the seeing of it is 'no-seeing'. Though we know ourselves, all the time a bad habit of the mind (adhyāsa) stands in the way of pure or free knowing, so that we never 'look' at it without tainting it.

To reach purity of self-knowing is the aim of the Zenist. The belief is that the I can look directly at the I. Although called intuition, it does not in this case imply something coming from anywhere or anything or anyone else. This is the supreme insight or perfect wisdom (prajñā pāramitā). Hence Hui-neng's objection to the simile of the mirror. (See under Hui-neng and Mirror.)

Seng-tsan. In Japanese, So-san (d.606). Third Zen Patriarch. Reputed author of a long and celebrated poem on the 'Believing Mind' (*Hsin-hsin-ming*), which is considered by many to be the first clear and comprehensive account of Zen in Chinese literature. The poem begins: 'The perfect Way (Tao) has no difficulty, except that it avoids preferences.' The first part of it ends, in Waley's translation: 'The struggle between for and against is the mind's worst disease.'

Its main theme is that the Perfect Way refuses to admit preferences; liking and disliking are diseases of the mind, which should rest serenely in the realization of the unity of all things. This being so, the mind is not disturbed by 'the ten thousand things'. Therefore avoid duality, even of subject and object, which is due to ignorance. Thus we come to know ourselves as what we really are; small or large, oneself or another, all are one, with no past, present or future.

It was also he who said that when all things (the 'ten thousand things') are viewed in unity, we are back at the Origin, where we always really were.

Sesshin, The. Also called Che-hsin. A week of specially long meditation which occurs once each month during April to August and October to February. During these weeks of sesshin, the manual labour of the monastery is reduced to a minimum. The meditation begins at 3 a.m. in the summer and 4 a.m. in the winter, and goes on till late at night, with intervals for eating, exercising and relaxation. The Roshi (Master) gives daily discourses and grants interviews. There is also a lecture every day, in connection with which two textbooks are particularly used, namely *Hekiganshu* (*q.v.*) and *Rinzairoku* (*q.v.*). There are also recitations of the Prajñā-pāramitā-hridaya-sūtra.

The word sesshin means literally the joining of mind to mind. During the session the students remain in the monastery and have not only meditations, but also tea-ceremonies, and koan-interviews. The koan-interview (*q.v.*) is individual and private.

Before the discourse, lights and flowers are arranged in front of the image of Buddha. The teacher makes his triple bow to the statue before beginning his discourse and then sits on a high chair facing it at the back of the room, while the students fold their books in cloths before putting them on the floor, out of reverence for them. The fourfold vow is then recited three times – the vows to save all living beings, to destroy all worldly passions, to enter the gates of dharma, and to fulfil the path to Buddhahood.

Shākyamuni. Literally, the sage of the Shākya clan. Refers to Buddha. The word muni, though frequently translated as sage, means a 'silent one'. This does not, however, refer to one who does not speak, who may be far from being a sage, but to one who really knows that which cannot be spoken.

Shen-hui (686–760). In Japanese, Kataku Jinne. A famous disciple of Hui-neng. He strongly promoted the doctrine of sudden enlightenment, to be reached by wu-nien (no-thought); especially must one not *think* of what is aimed at, e.g. enlightenment or nirvāna. The psychology of this is that in thinking of the goal one brings up one's old wrong conceptions and so prevents the attainment; so the aim (the pointing finger) is important, but the thought of the goal must be dropped. This is akin to what sometimes happens in ordinary life: one has in vain puzzled over the meaning of something, but suddenly understanding comes when one is not thinking of it. For the same reason Hindu teachers sometimes taught their students to meditate 'without desire', for the simple reason that their thoughts about it were wrong and would stand in the way of their success in the meditation.

After the deaths of Shen-shiu and Hui-neng, Shen-hui went north and effectively protested against the listing of Shen-shiu as Sixth Patriarch, so that a little later the name of Hui-neng was restored to that position, and Shen-hui's name put in as the seventh. In 753 he was exiled for being too exuberant in his public teaching, but a few years later he became restored to favour, being very useful on account of his eloquence – employed, it is said, in selling licences for admission to monkhood, on a large scale.

Shen-shiu. Jinshu, in Japanese (606–706). An instructor of monks at the monastery of Hung-jen, the Fifth Chinese Patriarch in Huang-mei in Hupei Province. He wrote a gāthā for the purpose of becoming the successor of Hung-jen, but that teacher did not find its sentiment a correct statement of Zen, and chose Hui-neng for the status. (See under Hui-neng.) Hui-neng left the area and formed the 'Southern School of Bodhidharma', while Shen-shiu remained, and was by many regarded as Sixth Patriarch after the death of Hung-jen. He suddenly became very prominent when the Empress Wu in the year 700 gave him a high position as 'Teacher to three Emperors'. He died in 706, and the list of Patriarchs was engraved on his tomb, with his name as Sixth, instead of that of Hui-neng.

Shih-tou. Sekito (*q.v.*).

Shikan-tanza. The sitting down which accompanies the practice of Saijo Zen.

Shin. An offshoot of the Pure Land or Jodo Sect (*q.v.*).

Shingon. The second largest sect of Buddhism in Japan, whose principal founder was Kobo Daishi. Sometimes referred to as the Mystical School. Not a Zen School.

Shinto and Zen. Traditions, allegories and symbols such as we find in Shinto, credited as containing inspiration to modes of cultural activity not based upon empirical knowledge, if valued and even worshipped by man, can prove themselves to be the treasury of his 'subconscious' or 'unconscious' potentiality.

Deep in man are the responses to these, when they are not looked upon and treated as individualistic instruments for personal gain. Let this Western modern 'madness' drop (at least in intuitive non-rational intervals) its material-welfare-seeking mood, and recognize the presence of a treasury of unknown 'goods', and it may put itself in the way of unfolding its so-far imprisoned subconscious treasury into a union of inner and outer in actual life.

It is in this matter that Zen finds in Japan a very living appeal, since the instinctive Shinto is open to what we may call the influences of the interior. In Zen, if faith is put as the first requirement, as it is, it is faith in the impending blossoming of the individual tree of life, not in more trunk and more leaves, but in a newness of life (beyond reason, which works with old and calcified facts) welcomed with loving warmth from the interior of the soul or self-nature of man.

That this, even if coldly regarded as an individual effort and ex-perience, supremely precious, can in its unfolding actuate universal love (the feeling of unity), and indeed require this for its success (as indicated in the Bodhisattwa vow), is so much the better for the *spirit* (not the interpretation, unless it be deeply psychological) of non-political Shinto, which permits, without any surrender of itself, as-sociation with the best of Buddhist or of Christian belief among its devotees and within its fold.

Shippe. A bamboo rod a few feet long, sometimes carried by Zen Masters either as insignia of authority or for demonstration purposes.

Shobogenzo. A work written by Dogen (*q.v.*).

Shojo Zen. A term applied to the meditation of the Theravādins of Ceylon, etc., having the aim of escape from the round of births and deaths. It is included within the term Mushinjo, and also sometimes used for self-induction of trance conditions.

Shore, The Other. A technical term by Buddha to indicate the reaching of enlightenment. In the Pure Land Sect it is believed that a 'bridge' can be built by others to help one cross to 'the other shore', but not so in Zen, nor in Theravāda.

Shorinji, The. In Chinese, Shao-lin, a temple on the Wu-t'ai Mountain to which Bodhidharma went and near which he meditated in a cave for nine years, after his failure to win the understanding and support of the Emperor Wu.

Shraddhotpāda Shāstra. See Awakening of Faith.

Shrāvaka. The meaning of the word is 'hearer'. It refers to the aspirant who is an ardent hearer of the words of Buddha, but more often a reader in our modern day of widespread literacy. It is taken for granted that 'hearing' is always followed by 'thinking over' or meditating, and still further, contemplation. The term is mostly used by the Theravādins, while the Mahāyānists think of the aspirant as a potential Bodhisattwa.

Shūnyatā. Literally, emptiness. Shūnya means void, and the suffix -tā is equivalent to the termination -ness in English.

This word is used to describe the essential nature of all things. As regards anything, it has been remarked by several Western thinkers, 'The whole is more than the sum of its parts.' That whole is some-thing new in nature – new in itself and new in its impact on other things. That whole also is not to be defined by any of the parts. In the concept and impact of that whole, there is an absence of the con-cept or impact of any part – 'form' part or 'quality' part. This fact applies to the smallest thing as well as to the greatest; it applies to the greatest material complex or to a chemical atom or even to an electron, so there are no basic wholes or ultimate particles, but there is only infinite divisibility, and, however small a whole, there are still parts, and still that whole has character – nature and impact – which cannot be found in any part.

Because of this the whole cannot be either known or defined or communicated or even conceived in terms of any part. Its nature is therefore *void* of any conception related to the parts. Its reality is a void. It is *sui generis*.

When the Zenist says that the true self-nature of man, or the true nature of oneself, is shūnyatā, he is enunciating a similar idea. He is careful to say that this true self-nature is not something additional to the object as seen by the eye or as known by the mind. Such addition to it would only be another part. The discovery of one's true self is therefore not merely the discovery of another part of oneself unknown or unnoticed before. It is 'that' of which this complex of parts is the embodiment. It is 'that' which has no parts.

This self-nature or shūnyatā is sometimes said by Zenists to be our Buddha-nature. Buddha means the wise, one who knows – knows the reality of himself and what he sees, knows the shūnyatā of imperfect seeing and imperfect knowing (that such is void of reality), and knows the shūnyatā of perfect seeing and knowing (that such is void of the imperfect).

That is why the Zenist will not regard the 'spirit' as a third kind of thing – the body being one, and the mind or 'soul' another. That is why he will not countenance the notions of a creator, or a creation. That is why he rejects a 'divine mind', as well as a 'divine form' – both being anthropomorphic. That is why in his Buddhism he will not accept the policy of 'escape from the sansāra' or wheel of births and deaths. That is why he rejects any sort of 'heaven' or 'pure land', but accepts Buddha's doctrine of Nirvāna. (See also Tathatā.) That is also why reality is void of anything or nothing; though both are real, they are not perfectly so. Hence it was said by Huang Po that the Void is both one and many, which are then, it must be added, non-separate. The Void is devoid of separates and of separateness. In other words reality contains both the somethings and the nothings, but taken separately these do not present reality, which is the summum genus. (See also under Void.)

Shuvjo. A staff used by Zen Masters to demonstrate the truth of Zen. The conventional idea about this is that it reminds the holder that if he knows a stick he knows all, and has reached Satori. A story is told that once, in an assembly of monks, someone asked Bokuju what statement could surpass those of Buddha and the Patriarchs. He replied, 'I call this a staff; what do you call it?' There was no answer, but Bokuju said he had answered the question. Many stories are told of statements by various Zen Masters with reference to the staff, which are devoid of all apparent reason or sense. Some people have thought that this device was resorted to for the purpose of shocking or startling the monks out of their mentalizing, or at least out of their previous notions.

For example, one Master said: 'When you know what this staff is your studies are finished.' Another: 'When you have a staff I will give it to you. When you have not, I will take it away.' Another: 'I call this a staff; what do you call it?' Another, after saying that one lion reveals millions of lions, and one speck of dust reveals the whole earth, lifted his staff and said: 'Here is my staff; where is that lion?' And so on.

Silence. Sometimes mere silence was used instead of exclamations or sticks, as in the case of Buddha's original conveyance of Zen to Māhakāshyapa. A similar case occurred when Basho Yesei was asked by a monk to show him the non-dual reality; the Master answered only by silence. Such silence was sometimes said to be 'like thunder', so impressive and effective was it. This is not to be confused with the Voice of the Silence (*q.v.*) which comes within the heart, not from a teacher. Incidentally, it should be remembered that in India and China the 'heart' (hridaya in Sanskrit) did not mean the organ for pumping blood as it does today, but the interior of the chest as a general region of the body, as the seat of good feelings.

Many are the recorded examples of a Teacher's silence in response to a question, but in many other cases there was what may be called 'avoidance', evidently intended to have the same effect. When asked about the self one Master replied that when there are clouds the moon cannot shine. In this one can detect a logical comparison, but not so easily in some other cases, such as when a monk requested his teacher to say how the silence could be expressed, and received the reply: 'At midnight last night I lost three pennies beside my bed.' Even this answer could carry a hidden reference to 'coverings of the light', even though the speaker may not have been intending that, since it could have been an involuntary response of the subconscious mind. This view, however, would dissatisfy some Zenists. Still, other cases, in which the Master remained silent for a time, would generally be considered more effective. Even an involuntary pause in the midst of a discourse sometimes sets the minds of an audience searching formlessly for the time being.

Sixth Sense. This term does not apply to Zen. It was invented long ago by the Hindus to refer to the mind which receives impressions from all the senses and coordinates them. Thus, e.g., when we look at a stone we know it is hard and solid, because of prior use of the sense of touch along with that of sight. A modern use of the term sixth sense applies it to the means of vision called clairvoyance, clair-audience, etc., but the Zenist Masters appear to have ignored these phenomena. Extra-sensory perception, the new term for these and cognate phenomena, does not mean totally outside or beyond the familiar five senses. Certainly, as regards the senses, and not the organs, clairaudience and clairvoyance would not be 'extra', because there is still audience and voyance, unless the conveyance in such cases is in some new sense-mode, and only translated into audience and voyance in the brain or in the mind. The strict Zenist will have no theory as to how his Satori comes.

Skandhas. As taught by Buddha, the five branches or components of the human so-called entity, which is really, however, a constantly changing conglomerate of form, emotion, perception, tendencies of character and mental discrimination. (See under Anatta.) This bundle of five it is which, undergoing constant modification, passes from incarnation to incarnation.

Some think of them as just going up and down in status until at some time there is an 'opening of the doors of the mind', followed by voluntary efforts to improve their condition and perhaps even to realize the truth. Others maintain that there is anyhow, through ordinary experience, a necessary constant improvement in them, because by any use of thought thought grows, and the same is true of all mental and moral faculties. They further insist that it must be so because one does not find a young infant or a very primitive man practising Zen, since it requires some mental maturity ('enough') to initiate the endeavour. This is quite another thing from the changing of one's *environment* from life to life by karma (*q.v.*).

Sokei. Hui-neng's temple, at Obai, near Canton.

Sosan. In Chinese, Seng-tsan. Third Chinese Zen Patriarch.

Soto. Tsao-tung, in Chinese. This sect of Zen was founded by Tsao Shan and his teacher Tung Shan, also known as the Zen Master Liang Chiai. The Japanese names for these are Sozan and Tozan; hence the word Soto. Tozan Ryokai, a contemporary of Rinzai, is also by many regarded as the very first founder. Hsing Szu carried it on after Tsao Shan and Tung Shan. Later, its teaching was taken to Japan by Dogen, who established the Soto Sect in Japan in 1227, where it flourished greatly and now has more than 15,000 temples. After Dogen, Kei-zan (1268–1325) did much to popularize Soto.

This sect does not use koans, but follows the gentle methods of the Mokusho Zen (*q.v.*), including the quiet cross-legged sitting in meditation which is called zāzen (*q.v.*).

Training in the Soto School follows a system of five stages, called the five relations. These are as between a prince and his minister, or a host and his guest. Prince or host stands for the spiritual reality which is our real being and real home. In contrast with it is minister or guest, the dependent or deluded or at any rate material and mental man, the person who finds himself in this world.

The first stage begins when one discovers or accepts the idea that there *is* a great spiritual reality, or that there is in oneself some sort of higher or superior self very much in contrast to this 'little self down here'. This superior self is called the prince or host, which comes very near to the idea of God as ruler or as the God within. Philosophically, it is the 'real' over-shadowing the 'seeming', and is represented by a circle in which a large dark (unseen or invisible or unknown) part looms over a smaller light (seen) part, thus: ●

The second stage begins when one recognizes and accepts the fact that one is a minister, that is, a servant of the prince, or acknowledges and welcomes the spiritual as one's master, or when one discovers that he is only a guest in the world and begins to think that he should act properly towards the host.

Now one begins to set aside personal desires and pleasures in order to serve the prince or the host. Philosophically, it is now the over-shadowing or higher and greater principle that is the light, that is the 'important thing' and the man who is dark, foolish, sinful and ignorant. So in the second diagram the positions are the same, but the colours are reversed, thus: ◐

A strong expression used in this second stage to describe the man is that he 'becomes like a withered log', as his attachments die away. No doubt this is how worldly people often regard the 'religious'.

In the third stage the 'withered log' blossoms again, for the real or spiritual now becomes an achievement in the world. There is now positive spiritual living, in place of the old negative responsiveness, which was shrivelled up in the second stage. This is called the up-coming of the real. The servant now feels that the higher or the real is really himself, in other words, that the real is within himself rather than above or beyond. Similarly, in the relation of host and guest the guest becomes more and more aware of the presence of the host, so that the host's interests are becoming his interests. This is depicted as the spirit within the man as follows: ⊙

As the Zenic meditative practice proceeds on these lines, the effect grows stronger and stronger, so that in the diagram the black spot of not-seeing diminishes as the minister or the guest becomes more and more luminous with the spirit. This involves an increasing wu-wei (*q.v.*) or response to the behests of the 'spirit' and corresponding decline of the mind. Its fulfilment should result in the constant awareness of the reality, so that the wu-wei is not suppression of mentality, but its decline as motivation, and even as basis of knowledge.

This leads on to the fourth stage. Here the picture is all light: ○ Now the guest is in all respects one with the host, or the minister one with the prince, so that there is no other motivation. This would show itself in ordinary life when the man has no longer any planning for his own separate self, but only proceeds with thinking or acting when there is a 'call'.

Then comes the fifth stage, represented by an all-black disc: ● Now the realization of oneness with the prince or with the host involves oneness with all, so that the realization includes everything, and even the seemingly erroneous or mayavic. After all, it was only the seeming that was wrong. To use expressions from a different sect, in the fourth stage 'the dewdrop slips into the shining sea', but in the fifth stage 'the universe grows I'.

These circle symbols are derived from Tsao Shan. The other co-founder of the Tsao-tung (Soto) Sect used a set of combinations of horizontal rods, short and long, after the manner of the old *Book of Changes* (*I Ching*).

For those who are familiar with the old *Book of Changes* it may be mentioned that the five combinations given are, in order, the 'Sun' and 'Tui' trigrams, and the 'Ta Kuo', 'Chung Fu' and 'Chung Li' hexagrams.

Southern School. When Hui-neng (Wei-lang in Southern dialect) was inducted into the Patriarchate, the Fifth Patriarch advised him to leave the place lest someone do him harm, conducted him personally to Kiu-kiang, saw him across the river, and left him there, whence he proceeded southward. After various adventures he arrived at Canton, where the monk Yen-chung (Yin-tsing) invited him to a seat of honour at the Fa-shing temple, where he stayed and preached. The Sixth Patriarch inherited the robe at the age of 24, was ordained at 39, and died at 76. His teaching in the south came to be known as the Southern School of Zen.

Sozan. Tsao Shan, in Chinese. (See under Soto.)

Sticks. Those used by Zen Masters were of two kinds: the larger one (called the shippe) which he used for support, and for striking his disciples and visitors; the shorter staff (called the hossu) for gesturing and ceremonial purposes.

As a kind of insignia of office, the latter was often used to draw attention when the Master was about to make a pronouncement, and prepare the monks' minds for what was coming, by this indicating that his spiritual function was now active. This would have been the case, e.g., when one of them asked the Master Ling-yen a question. The Master raised up his hossu and then gave his response. Another example: one day the Master Huang-po Hsi-yun ascended his high seat, took up his staff and drove all the monks out. Then he called them and said something about the moon. He had impressed them with the importance of what he was going to say. This staff, however, was also used with certain significance, as, e.g., when the Master Yen Tou hid it behind his back it was understood that his spiritual function had returned to rest.

That the hossu could be identical with the fly-whisk is shown in one story where the word is used. A young man was bent upon a military career as a swordsman; nevertheless he had gone to a Zen Master for some advice. The Master, seeing that his proper destiny was the monkhood, challenged him to a fight on condition that he was to become a monk if he lost. For the fight he was to use a bamboo rod, and the master his fly-whisk (hossu). The young man failed to strike the Master even once, but the Master dusted his face with the fly-whisk again and again.

It seems that this implement was originally only a fly-whisk, composed of a stick about a foot long, with a ring at one end for hanging it up, and a long tuft of horse or yak hair at the other end.

It should be mentioned that an ordinary stick (called the keisaku, warning stick) was used in monasteries during group meditations to bring to order any who might be sitting crooked or dozing, who were then expected to bow politely and mend their ways.

Stories. The following are well-known specimens of Zen stories, much condensed:

Two monks, one older, one young, came to a muddy ford where a pretty girl was waiting to cross. The elder picked her up and carried her over the water. As they walked along, the younger, horrified at the act of his brother monk in touching a woman, kept on commenting upon it, until at last the elder exclaimed, 'What! Are you still carrying that girl? I put her down as soon as we crossed the water.'

When a Master was troubled by a monk who persisted in saying that he could not understand, the Master said, 'Come nearer.' The monk came nearer. The Master again said, 'Come nearer,' and once more the monk did so. 'How well you understand!' remarked the Master.

A boastful monkey went to heaven and there met Buddha. He said, 'Buddha is a small thing, but I can jump many leagues.' 'If you are so clever,' said Buddha, 'jump away from the palm of my hand.' The monkey thought that would be easy, since the palm seemed to him only inches wide. So he leaped far, far away. He found himself on a large plain bounded by five great pillars. To prove he had been there he made a mark at the base of one of these. After returning to Buddha he boasted of what he had done. 'But look at my hand,' said Buddha. There the monkey saw the mark which he had made. It was at the base of one of Buddha's fingers.

A Master was once approached by a boy requesting instruction, so the Master gave him the koan, 'What is the sound of the clap of one hand?' The boy went away and happened to hear some Geishas playing music, so he went to the Master and imitated that. On being told that was not it, he went away and heard water dripping, again the wind blowing, again the locusts – altogether ten times. All were wrong. Then the boy could find or think of no more, and lo! he discovered the soundlessness of one hand, the sound of sound.

A man chased by a tiger jumped over a cliff and clung to a tree growing on the side. Looking down, he saw another tiger waiting for him to fall. Worse and worse, he saw two mice, one white, one black, gnawing at the branch to which he was clinging. It chanced that he just then caught sight of some strawberries growing within reach. With one hand he plucked a strawberry and put it in his mouth. 'How good that tastes,' he thought.

A Zen monk named Ryokan lived in a hut, alone and without any possessions. One day when he was out, a thief entered, to steal. He was about to depart when the monk returned. The monk said, 'I am sorry you have found nothing; please take my clothes.' After the thief had gone, the monk sat naked, looking at the moon. 'Alas,' he mused, 'what a pity that I could not give him that beautiful moon.'

Struggle. The zenic endeavour is never as a simple growth. It requires very strenuous effort, which goes, however, not into the final attainment, but to the task of directing one's attention to the right aim, notwithstanding old impulses or habits in the body, emotions or mind which arouse other desires than that of the one great achievement. This does not imply severe austerity, but as much of what may seem austerity to the self-indulgent as to establish peace and health in the body, emotions and mind, or else that state of the man's own conscious power which leaves him undiverted from his purpose even while he is conscious of the nagging disturbances. This includes the disturbances from material objects, from other people, and from one's own past, and also, as far as this goal is concerned, disturbances from opinions or ideas. Questions such as what may happen after death should not come up. They are of no importance; what is important is what is here, now, and in what manner the man will face it. The will is all-important, not the opinion. It is related of a certain Zen Master that when someone asked, 'What is Zen?' he replied, 'Boiling oil over a blazing fire.'

Subject and Object. Rinzai's 'four arrangements' for consideration of this relation form an ascending series, not unlike that of the 'Lord and vassal' of the Soto Sect. (1) Leave out the object and meditate on the subject only. (2) Leave out the subject and meditate on the object only. (3) Leave out both subject and object and meditate only on . . . (4) Eliminate the elimination.

We could theorize and say, 'Thus find reality,' but reality would then become a new object of meditation! The aim is to realize the prajñā, but the method of Zen meditation is to do, not to have an aim in view. Similarly, in Patanjali's samādhi, or contemplation, there is to be no aim, no desire, because the yogi does not know beforehand what he is going to experience. So also with satori; it is not an object aimed at, not even a subjective object; but a new experience, and yet 'a new experience' cannot be the aim, for the very thought of experience will nullify the possibility.

Sudden School. A formula of the Rinzai Sect of Zen, in reference to the suddenness with which Mahākāshyapa received the teaching from Buddha. This sect holds that the enlightenment must always be sudden, and cannot be approached by degrees. There are 6,000 Rinzai temples in Japan. The Rinzai texts cover a wide field of Chinese texts and translations from Sanskrit. Rinzai Zen was also called, in China, Lin Chi School. This school uses koans (q.v.).

The Sudden School movement was greatly promoted by Shen-hui, an immediate disciple of Hui-neng, in strong contrast to the gradual school of Shen-hsiu.

Sukhāvatī. See under Pure Land Sect.

Sumiye. Japanese ink painting. (See under Artistry and Arts of Zen.)

Surangama Sūtra. Called *Leng Yen Ching*, in China. This was brought to China by the great Indian monk Paramārtha about 517, and translated by him into Chinese with the aid of Wang Yung, formerly a Minister of State. This work took about two years. It angered the Emperor that this had been done without first securing the permission of the Government, so Wang Yung was punished and Paramārtha was forced to return with his manuscript to India.

No one knows how the Chinese translation of the Sūtra was preserved. In the course of time, however, it came to be tremendously valued by Chinese Buddhists and Taoists (as it was by Indian Mahāyāna Buddhists) as in it Buddha describes the steps to be taken and the meditation to be undertaken to reach the great Enlightenment – describing the tranquillizing of the mind by exclusion of concepts arising directly and indirectly from sensory experiences, the nature of the Truth realized in the samādhi or deepest contemplation, and the transcendental virtues and powers resulting. Finally, it treats of the highest perfect wisdom, anuttara-samyak-sambodhi (q.v.).

Sympathy. The Zen attentiveness to Nature is very close to the old idea of sympathy. There is an expression which one used often to hear in India: 'I do like Mr So-and-So; he is so very sympathetic.' Sympathy did not here mean considerateness towards suffering, but similarity of feeling, the ability to put oneself in another's place and share his point of view, fellow-feeling.

There was an old man in India who used to spend his days sitting at the roadside near to a rich man's gate, and there receive the gratuities of the passers-by. Sometimes the gate would open and the rich man or some of his family would emerge into the road, riding in a stately carriage with beautiful horses, a driver and a groom. One day when this occurred a passer-by spoke to the old man sympathetically (as he thought): 'It must be very galling to you to sit here in your poverty and infirmity, and see that rich man go out like that in his carriage.' 'You sympathize with me,' replied the old man, 'I sympathize with that rich man.' 'Whatever do you mean?' exclaimed the 'Samaritan'. 'He is happy, is he not?' was the reply. 'I enjoy his happiness. I should be sad if he were in trouble.' This was good Zen. It is what made Emerson write in one of his poems, 'I am the owner of the sphere, etc.'

T

T'ang Dynasty (618–907). This period has been called the golden age of Zen. Nevertheless there was a severe persecution of Buddhists in China in 845, from which only Zen survived with any great strength. Following this were five feeble dynasties, up to 960, when the great Sung dynasty began, with its splendid development of literary activity and the establishment of libraries. This lasted until 1278.

Tao-an (d.385). Scholar and monk. Textual editor and commentator, just prior to Kumārajīva. Was especially interested in presenting the yoga methods of Indian Buddhism in their application to Taoism. His most noted disciple was Hui-yuan (*q.v.*).

Tao-hsin. In Japanese, Doshin (579–651). Fourth Zen Patriarch. In his time there was a schism – one branch, headed by Fa-jung (*q.v.*), soon died out; the other was led by Hung-jen (*q.v.*) who became the Fifth Patriarch.

Tao-hsuan. Compiler of the *Biographies of the Zen Masters*.

Tao-i. Ma-tsu (*q.v.*).

Taoism. The old religion of China acquired the term Tao Chia (School of Tao) in the Shih Chi historical recording of about 97 B.C. It is generally considered to have been formulated by the sage Lao Tsu in the fourth century B.C. According to tradition, the book *Tao Te Ching* was dictated to Yin-hi, a border official, by Lao-tsu when he was leaving for an unknown destination.

The movement is related to the later Zen Buddhism by its emphasis on tranquillity, non-artificiality, simple enlightenment and especially by its doctrine of wu-wei (*q.v.*).

Tao-sheng (360–434). A distinguished pupil of Kumārajīva and Hui-yuan. He maintained that all people can attain Liberation because all have the Buddha-nature. This view was unpopular but was supported by the *Mahāparanirvāna Sūtra* when it came to light. It is held by the Tien-tai, Pure Land and Zen schools. He also emphasized the doctrine of abrupt or sudden enlightenment, which became very strong in the T'ang dynasty, especially in the Zen schools. He denied and opposed the old view that man had a 'soul', above what we may call his ordinary constitution, and that this was his Buddha-nature.

Tao, The. Has been described as formless, nameless, the motive of all movements and the mother of all substances. With all that, it has an original nature of its own, called the Teh, the virtue of it – virtue not only in the modern sense of being true to one's status (that is, e.g., the human being takes care not to lower his status into an animal condition by surrendering to bodily impulses instead of living according to intellectual and moral ones). This Teh has also been called virile harmony, inasmuch as the degree of its presence marks the virility or strength of all the human faculties and the vitality of the body, and also harmonious relations with all beings and things.

Tao with its Teh causes the man to tread the proper way, which again is itself the Tao or Path (dhamma or dharma, in Buddhism). The Tao is thus also the true 'way of going'. This can be seen in the facts that truth is truth and love is love; there are no degrees in truth or love. Love is either love or it is not; if selfishness (anti-harmony), however subtle, is there, it is not love. The Teh could thus be said to be the same as 'the light that lighteth every man that cometh into the world'.

This view gives rise to a certain explanation of vitality as health. In the body, if the natural laws are properly obeyed mentally so that it is not polluted by bad thoughts from within, the harmony of this relationship allows the 'God within' to be present in the form of health or vitality. From this proceeds the fact that the feeling of health or the experience of health is the awareness of the divine (self-existent and self-shining) in the body, in brief, the Tao or the Teh.

The same idea applies socially in the very difficult problem presented by Buddhism in general when it preaches the giving up of desire. To give up personal motives (kalpana) is to live with the motive of only response to others, not selfishness (separateness) – that is, according to Tao and Teh. So Lao-tsu could say: 'Tao undertakes no activity, yet nothing is left undone.' In this there is 'no interference and no assertion' (wu-wei).

It is because the Tao and the wu-wei are so identifiable with the 'Buddha-mind' and the 'void' (shūnyatā) and the principle tathatā (suchness) that Zen is so acceptive of Tao-ism, at least the part of it which does not rely upon rites and ceremonies, which are very contrary to Buddha's teaching.

Tao-te-ching. A very famous Chinese philosophical and mystical treatise, attributed to the Chinese philosopher Lao-tsu. (See under Lao-tsu, the Tao and Taoism.)

Tao-yuan. Compiler of *The Transmission of the Lamp*.

Tāriki. The doctrine of 'other-effort', or salvation by faith and grace. This is the characteristic of the Jodo and the Jodo-Shin, found in the

Schools and Temples of the Pure Land Sect. This idea is not approved by strict Zenists. It contrasts with jiriki.

Tathāgata. A name by which Buddha frequently referred to himself. It may be made up of tathā (meaning 'in that manner') and gata (gone), alluding to the fact that he himself had trodden the way or path which he was describing to his followers, that he knew what he was talking about and was not simply passing information along.

The term has been understood in several ways. One is: 'He who has gone in that manner (tathā)', that is, who has trodden the path which he announced and taught. Another: 'He who has come from the suchness', that is, back from the tathatā after reaching enlightenment. Another: 'He who is the very suchness itself'. The last is given in the scripture entitled Vajrachchhedika. The present writer favours the first of these explanations, because the first part of the word is tathā (in that manner), *not* tathatā (suchness), which latter would make it tathatāgata, meaning 'come from the suchness'.

Tathatā. Literally, 'That-way-ness.' Usually translated 'suchness'. The word tathā means 'in that manner', or, coming after yathā (which means 'just as'), it can be translated 'so also' or 'just so'. The 'tā' at the end of the word has the significance of the affix 'ness' in English.

This is the essential description of what a thing is, but it is non-descriptive in that it does not compare the thing with anything else, but simply refers us back to the thing, saying in effect, 'That is what *it* is.' It means the fact of something being what *it* is, quite different from anything else, just as Jehovah is reputed to have described himself as 'I am what *I* am' – implying 'not what something else is', as is easily seen if the emphasis is placed on the second 'I'. Our real self-nature is not what is seen by the mind.

We may say of a man that he is not to be known by any of his parts, and yet the true man or self-nature is not another part, usually unseen. The whole is not the sum of the parts and yet it gives value to the parts. It is as though there were a function-power 'incarnated' by means of the organic unity of the structures or parts. This 'suchness' it is that raises the zenic illumination or experience of self-nature beyond mere mysticism, which refers to what one sees 'with the eyes closed', and even without the eyes of the mind.

Tathatā has therefore been called by some the 'thatness' of anything, by others 'is-ness', by others the 'suchness' and by some just the nature of the thing, as in 'the self-nature of man'. It has also been affirmed that emptiness (shūnyatā) is suchness and suchness is emptiness, because the suchness of anything is devoid of any other thing.

That everything has fundamental 'suchness' may be indicated by the illustration of gravitation. All things, say from A to Z, are affected by the others, but according to their own nature. If A is attracted or influenced by B to Z, then B is influenced by A and C to Z, so while A is influenced by 25 others it also influences 25 others, and thus it has a share of the *original power* or *nature*. What that nature is no mind can tell; mind can only see A–Z and their mutual reactions. Their essential nature it cannot see.

If the term God, divested of all anthropomorphism, is used for the original power of self-being or self-nature, then the Eastern view has always been that man can know God by overcoming the impurity which his mind imposes on his seeing. In this seeing he is not man (from the Sanskrit verbal root, 'man', to think), so it is still true that 'no *man* hath seen God at any time.' One can understand also why it was said of the little children also, 'In heaven their angels always behold the face of the Father,' followed by the at first sight unconnected statement, 'I come to restore that which was lost.' A Zenist might say that this referred to the seeing of the self-nature, and that in this matter Jesus was a good Zenist.

It is prajñā that realizes 'suchness' (tathatā), the void, self-nature, etc. It is to be distinguished from sanjñā which is mental, being consciousness of objects or 'others'.

Tea Ceremony. In Japanese, cha-no-yu. The word ceremony is not correctly applied to this, for there is no set form to be achieved, unless it can be said that the avoidance of achievement is the skill and form of the occasion. Entering into meditation also is not to be ranked as either an achievement or an attainment. The tea ceremony, because it is an outward form productive of or conducing to an inward peace of self-being, living without coping with any thing or things, is the form of either overcoming them or obtaining release from them. The appointments, equipment and surroundings of the occasion (see under Tea Room) should not be stereotyped or admirable (admire-able), nor represent any achievement or accomplishment, unless the getting away from accomplishment and the simplicity of non-effort – a situation requiring no adjustment or adaptiveness – be that.

Notwithstanding these essential principles, there grew up a great deal of 'correctness' with reference to all the details of equipment and procedure, so much so that by the sixteenth century more than a hundred rules were formulated. All these were, however, methods for naturalness, paradoxical as that may sound, but well understandable when we consider the unnatural habits and thoughts from which the guests are intended to be relieved. This useful paradox (so typically zenic) is well indicated by one of the rules, which states that he who wishes to proceed in the 'Way of Tea' must be his own teacher. It usually works out that there is a depression in the floor for the fire; over this is an iron kettle for boiling the water, which when ready is ladled into the drinking bowl. Next some green tea which has been finely powdered is spooned into the bowl and well stirred into the water with a tea-whisk. This is then handed to the guest, who sips the beverage little by little. At first the guests usually quietly converse on some artistic or philosophic topic, then stop talking and listen to the kettle 'singing', and afterwards they sip their tea.

Tea Room, The. This piece of architecture is considered to be specially related to Zen, because of the mood it helps to induce. First there is the frugality of it, which separates it even from the simple form and furnishings of the ordinary Japanese home. In its over-all features – thatched roof, simple walls, irregular ceiling, rough woodwork, low door, ten-foot-square floor space – it tends to the feeling of peaceful being and away from disturbing objects and thoughts. It is set off a little way from the dwelling-house, which is replete with thoughts of coping with things. The 'tea-things' should be the simplest, not arousing thoughts of achievement or coping of any kind. The path that leads to it should go through a piece of garden that represents simple nature and no achievement or attachment. All this does not conduce to somnolence but to contentment, while the tea itself is of a taste not concerned with either stimulation or relief. The whole situation conduces to 'man being in a state of peace', neither coping nor resting from coping.

The Tea Masters were considered to have been so well inducted into the spirit of Zen (in Buddhistic terms), or into the harmony of 'heaven and earth', or spirit and vesture of body (in terms of Tao), that their advice was sought and applied in all the arts of architecture and painting.

Teh. See under Tao.

Tendai School. In China, Tien-tai. This school was founded by Chich-che Tai-shih, or, briefly, Chih-i. Dr D. T. Suzuki regards this as a form of Zen, started independently of the line of Bodhidharma, but the followers of the School do not like this view, because the School now lays more emphasis on philosophy than on the practice of meditation.

The Tendai doctrine speaks of a threefold Truth, the three being three-in-one. These are (1) the truth that all things are of the Void, because they are dependents in the stream of causation and thereby not things-in-themselves, (2) the truth that the phenomenal existences of all kinds are only temporary productions and so only the Void – not real or self-existent, (3) that as everything involves everything else, all is one, and something of everything is the basis of its being, this something being the Buddha-nature.

Because of this item the School maintains that there is 'salvation for all', but not by either production or destruction of the characters or qualities of anything. The doctrine was based upon the Lotus Sūtra

(Saddharma-pundarīka) and the School is therefore called also the Lotus School. In China it is very popular and is often combined with the Pure Land Sect. It was carried to Japan in 804 by Dengyo Daishi.

Thanks. When a merchant gave 500 yen to the Ekakuji Temple in Kamakura, the Zen Master Seistan merely said, 'You have done a good deed.' It was like saying, 'Virtue is its own reward,' and anything like thanks may have savoured of rudeness, as perhaps implying that the donor was thinking of himself. Similarly, when an old-fashioned mendicant in India receives a gift, he says 'Santosham', meaning that he is pleased, and assuming, no doubt, that it was for that purpose that the gift was made and thus the donor will be happy.

Theravāda. Literally, the doctrine of the Elders in Buddhism. A form of Buddhism prevalent in Ceylon, Burma, Thailand, etc., which is not approved by Zenists, though regarded by them as an authentic teaching of Buddha but intended for the weaker brethren who are not up to the Zen effort.

Theravādin. One who follows the teaching and methods of the school of thought or system of Buddhism based upon the doctrine of the Elders formulated at the first Council after the death of Buddha. This branch of Buddhism is often called the Southern School of India, which is now to be found mostly in Ceylon, Burma, Thailand and Indonesia. The term Hinayāna (lesser way) is sometimes used, but this the Theravādins do not like, as it carries a feeling of slightingness in comparison with Mahāyāna Buddhism, which is the Northern School (of India), now found in Tibet, China and Japan. Zen arose in the teachings of the Northern School, but acquired such an adaptation to the concrete Chinese character and spirit of Tao, and later to the Japanese character of active concreteness, that it may be now said to be a school of its own.

Tien-tai School. See under Tendai.

Tokusan Senkan. Teh-shan Hsuan-chien (782–865). A great student of and believer in the scriptures, especially the Diamond Sūtra and the Prajnā-pāramitā. He doubted very much the possibility of the sudden and direct seeing of one's own Buddha-nature, but the fame of the Southern School caused him to go and see it for himself. He met the Master Ryotan Soshin (Lung-t'an). When the Master suddenly blew out the candle and so put him in complete darkness, he suddenly attained enlightenment, which affected him so much that he burnt his scriptures the next day.

Later, in the teaching of his followers he was noted for the use of the staff, with which he used to gesture whenever he addressed the gatherings of students. It is from him that came the threat – or was it a promise? – 'Whether you can answer or not, you will get thirty blows of the stick.'

He maintained that enlightenment can be gained from ordinary things, via complete emptiness (shūnyatā), concerning the subjective as well as the objective. He was also the author of a very effective statement, translated by Ruth Sasaki as follows: 'Only when you have no thing in your mind and no mind in things are you vacant and spiritual, empty and marvellous.'

There is an interesting story bearing upon Tokusan's conversion to Zen. On his way to visit Soshin, he came to a roadside tea-house and asked for refreshment. The woman in charge asked him what was in his bundle, and when he replied that it was commentaries on the Diamond Sūtra she told him, to his great surprise, that she had read in that Sūtra that the mind is not obtainable in the past, the present or the future, so she wished to know which mind of his he wished to refresh. With all his learning, he could not answer, so he went on his way baffled and somewhat shaken in his opposition to Zen. The puzzle turns upon the fact that the word for refreshment in Chinese is tien-hsin, and hsin is the mind.

Tozan (10th century). Tung Shan, in Chinese.

Tozan Ryokai. See under Soto.

Transmission of the Lamp. In full, 'The Records of the Transmission of the Lamp.' It was compiled A.D. 1004 by Tao-yuan. It is the earliest history of Zen still existing. Among other things it records the names of the 28 Indian Meditation School Patriarchs and the gāthās (verses) recited at the times of transmission. It is one of the two principal sources of early Zen history in China, the other being *Biographies of the High Priests* which was compiled in 645 by Tao-hsuan.

Tsao Shan. See under Soto.

Tsao Tung Sect. Soto, in Japanese. Founded by Pen Chi of Ts'ao Shan (Sozan) and Liang Chiai of Tung Shan (Tozan). (See under Soto.)

T'uan Chi. Huang Po (*q.v.*).

Tung Shan. See under Soto.

U

Ummon Bunen (d.949). Also known as Yun-men. The story of his loss of one leg is as follows. When he went to see the Zen Master Mokuju Dosho, who had been a disciple of Rinzai, the Teacher required first to know his name, and then urgently demanded: 'Who are you? Speak! Speak!' When Ummon (then known as Bun-yen or Wen-yen) hesitated, the Master pushed him violently through the gate, calling him a good-for-nothing fellow. The gate, in shutting, caught and broke one of Ummon's legs, but he afterwards considered the enlightenment he obtained from the experience to be well worth the pain and loss of a leg.

This story is taken as an illustration of the way in which something violent or unusual is needed to jolt the seeker out of his routine of ignorance or of ignorant explanations. This thought no doubt dominated Ummon's method of teaching later on, and led to his penchant for one-word or exclamatory answers, which came to be called 'one-word barriers'. Though he followed the lead of Rinzai, he always preferred the exclamation 'Kan!' or 'Kwan!' to Rinzai's way of giving a loud shout. It is to Ummon that we owe the well-known expression 'Walk on.' This was the reply he gave when asked, 'What is the Tao?' It was Ummon who when asked what the Tao is answered, 'Walk on.' It is related also that he wanted his followers to be very clear and definite in what they were doing, and to illustrate this said: 'When you sit, sit; when you walk, walk.'

Later, in his monastery of Ummon (from which he derived the name Ummon), he got a very large following. This was towards the end of the T'ang period, and during the five short dynasties which followed it.

Ummon Zen Sect. Also called Yun-men Sect. Founded by Wen-yen of Yun-men. It has now died away. It had three 'gates' or questions through which one could direct oneself to the main purpose. These were mainly concerning that which 'contains' all things, and the realization of mind as all, which puts an end to the series of rebirths.

Unconscious, The. In the Western terminology this is not intuition, but is that part of the product of mind which has gone into a sort of storehouse, and may come up again, sometimes with impelling or persistent force, in appropriate circumstances. It has by some been identified with 'lapsed intelligence', which is similar to the formation of structure in the body, by which in fact every joint and organ, though arising because of the response to environment of the living organism and its resultant adaptation, has become formed and settled by habit. The same process acting somehow in the mind gives us the subconscious, meaning what has fallen below the threshold of consciousness but is still there as a sort of structure or mental form. Instead of calling this 'subconscious', or 'lapsed intelligence', it has become usual to call it the unconscious, because it has lapsed below the threshold of consciousness.

All this, however, is quite different from the use of the word unconscious in Zen literature. Here it means that which is conscious of no object, not even of itself *as object*. It has also been called pure consciousness. It may also be spoken of as 'consciousness as such'. The danger of misunderstanding when it is called by such a term as 'suchness' is that even an abstract idea is objective to the mind. Since our consciousness is normally the consciousness of consciousness, that consciousness of which we are conscious is not consciousness pure and undefiled. Since, however, we are not conscious of unconsciousness, the consciousness that is unconscious of any object of consciousness, even of itself as such, has been called the unconscious (unconscious of anything, even the idea of consciousness). This is somewhat akin to the deep sleep state (sushupti) of Hindu philosophy. It is beyond dream. When you wake from it, you say, 'I slept well.' This is considered to be a memory, though undefinable, of a non-dual experience, for you do not say, 'I feel well after that sleep, so I infer that I must have slept well.' The same philosophy speaks of a turiya or fourth state, and this is no doubt the state realized by the Zenist who has reached to the perfect wisdom, Prajna. It is easy to see the consanguinity of the two terms, unconsciousness and emptiness (wu-hsin and shunyata).

The principle of the unconscious or the subconscious which is operative in Japanese Painting and Poetry (see under Arts of Zen) is central also in zenic action, as well indicated in the skill of archery. The art is forgotten but the skill remains, and the skill is felt in the act. In this there is a unity of the skill with the feeling (not the thought) of being, which makes the action pure. The fruit of the past is in the being of the actor, and not in his memory. In painting it is not that by the speed of the brush of the artist or in archery the swiftness of the pull and let-go that the 'unconscious' or 'no-thought' comes in. It is that in the union of all the past in the present action there is a consummation which has no parts. What is a new man but a union of all his past, which is the very incarnation of something greater than the parts, and which both in the feeling of being and in the acts of being is at its best when that unfinished business called memory is finished and dead? The Zenist integrates as he goes along.

Unity. See One-ness.

Upāya. Literally, 'means'; methods or devices. These, such as *mondos* and *koans* are used by many Zenists, as coming within the formula of Zen 'without the use of scripture, ritual or vow'.

V

Vajrachchhedika Sūtra, The. A portion of the Prajnāpāramitā literature which in the time of Hui-neng began to be preferred to the Lankavatāra Sūtra, as being simpler, more in keeping with the Tao, and much concerned with the idea of the Void (shūnyatā). It is often spoken of in English as the Diamond Sūtra (q.v.).

Vijnāna. Perceiving with mental knowledge. Different from prajnā, which is 'seeing' without mental knowledge, beyond both senses and mind.

Virtues or Perfections. Pāramitās (q v.).

Voice of the Silence. An expression used by some Mahāyāna Buddhists in referring to the intuition that comes to the meditator when his ordinary mind becomes silent. The dauntless energy which then carries him forward – the will which goes on when the thinking ceases – has then to be purified of all egotistic elation, and the 'voice' will then direct him. The further going must have its promotion from 'the inner light' (another figure of speech), not from what has gone on previously. In China the 'Divine Voice of the Self' refers to Kwan-yin.

Void, The. When we say that mind is a void we mean it is void of the meditations of objects, not devoid of objects. Objects in the mind are there in plenty, but we call them memories of objects or thoughts of objects or ideas of objects. But one must not mistake these mind-pictures for real external objects – that would be delusion.

'In the space of the mind', as the expression is, we can handle these mental pictures as easily as ever, move them about, arrange them in patterns, try new combinations, and view the effects. The young pair get married and go to the furniture store, and you may hear them talking: 'What if we put this couch under the window and that dresser against the opposite wall, and . . .' 'No, perhaps that would fit better or look better in the corner, especially if the curtains are of a pale coral colour.' And so on. What a task it would be if all those things had to be actually moved into all those positions to be viewed! And if at last the proposed arrangement does have to be tried out before acceptance, that is only because the mind is not yet perfect of its kind, strong, steady and quiet. At any rate the mind is a void or empty space in which objects voided of their objectivity may be viewed, felt, heard, smelt, and even tasted.

If the objects in fact are also voids it is because each of them by 'occupying space' voids the others, so that they may rightly be called voidings or voidances. Each is what it is because it excludes the rest, and is to that extent a factual, though not a perfect or complete, 'operation void'. 'Matter is that which occupies space.' Thus the perfect void, which is fundamental, stamps its character on all creation.

Let us then contemplate a further step – the voiding of mind. This zenic void will avoid mind-reality as well as matter-reality. Words and thoughts cannot reach into this, but consciousness can, knowing can. Thus the watchword of the Zenist who knows *of* this insight, this prajnā, and also something *about it* (as we have shown), is: 'Go on; go on; try; try.' First there is faith that it is, then there is doubt as to what it is, and then there is great perseverance. This is no shallow 'not this', for the not in that is a this of thought and thus there is 'not not' – even the not has to be excluded in the negation or wu (*q.v.*). The student is told not to be discouraged, but to face the right way and go on with faith. In the old proverb, 'Ripe fruit will not remain upon the bough.' (See also under Shūnyatā, Wu-nien, etc.)

W

Wang-wei (698–759). Famous artist, who wrote a biographical epitaph of Hui-neng, at the request of Shen Hui, the disciple of Hui-neng who vindicated his status.

Wei-shih School. See under Hsuan Tsang.

Wisdom and Knowledge. The word knowledge (jñāna) includes all kinds of knowledge in the three departments – knowledge about things (objects), knowledge about mind or life (subjects) and knowledge of the beyond, the supreme or the divine. Still, it is so often used in the world for scientific or objective knowledge that the religions have taken mostly to the use of the word 'wisdom' in connection with their meditations.

Wisdom, it may be noticed, takes life into account, and so goes beyond scientific knowledge, and enters the field of ethic. Thus: 'What is the use of a spade?' 'For digging.' 'But what is the digging for?' It must be for the benefit of somebody, so when things are known or valued in relation to life the word wisdom (or buddhi) is often used. Hence, some have translated buddhi as 'the higher intelligence'.

Beyond this is the 'perfect wisdom', prajñā, which in Zen is the knowledge of the 'Buddha-mind'. The seeking of knowledge implies a desire. One does not seek to know more about anything unless one is interested in it (for some reason). To be interested in life is the basis of love or ethic, and of the knowledge which is wisdom. (See also under Prajñā.)

Wisdom, Vertical and Horizontal. The 'vertical' is that penetrating insight which leads to knowing the thing as it is (the tathatā), and so goes upward, as it were, to the higher understanding or rather realization. The 'horizontal' is that which leads to knowing all about something. It is common in human learning and thinking for people to reach a certain level of knowledge and then go on elaborating and enlarging at that level, whereas in Zen meditation the aim is not to elaborate but to penetrate.

Words. 'One picture is worth a thousand words,' is an old Chinese saying. The reason for this is, no doubt, that the picture is there 'all at once', while words are strung out, and sometimes they are in the end 'lost in the desert' and do not even wearily 'wind their way to the sea'.

Worldly Winds, the Eight. These fan the passions: gain and loss; defamation and eulogy; praise and ridicule; sorrow and delight.

Worlds, the Three. Described as of (1) desire, (2) form and (3) formlessness. These are all in the sansāra, or region of births and deaths, the Void being other (para) than these.

When it is asked how the formless (arūpa) can be within the sansāra, we are referred to abstract thought, which occupies no space and has no extensity (rūpa, form), and yet has variety, definite contents and scope. Creation is regarded as coming about by reduction, not by production. Reduce the formless, or select something out of the abstract, and you have rūpa (a form) – for example, beauty (formless) and *a* beauty (form). Again, select among forms and you are limited by desire.

Everything is thus from the potential, not built from nothing or an imaginary collection of so-called atoms. It is that 'potential' which is the substance of all.

It is because of this 'potential' that Zen meditation requires complete control of thought and desire, or freedom from having one's consciousness controlled, occupied and limited by thoughts and desires. The Zenist does not avoid the three worlds, but does not let them bind him.

In modern psychology there is an increasing realization of the power of abstract over concrete – for example, thoughts of health or of disease affecting bodily functions.

Wu. See under Wu-wei and Wu-nien.

Wu-hsin. See under Wu-nien.

Wu-nien. Literally, 'no-thought'. Applied to meditation without thought or, in meditation on one's self-nature (*q.v.*), no-mind. This is not taken to imply a condition of consciousness excluding mind-operation, except in two ways. There is to be exclusion of mind-operation in the special meditation on self-nature. Then, one who has realized his own pure self-nature can with that nature of his know directly the self-nature of others and other things. This knowing of the essential nature of objects must not be tainted by mind, but will not exclude the mental seeing of the mind-qualities-nature and action-nature of things seen. It will only add to that an insight into their essential nature. So, just as mind and body can act together in mutual unity in their sphere of being, mind not preventing body operation, now self, mind and body can act together in mutual unity, self not preventing mind and body operation.

So, according to Hui-neng, wu-nien is not unconsciousness, but it is to see and to know things with the mind free from attachment. 'It pervades all, but sticks nowhere.' This is called thoughtlessness or idealessness (wu-nien). This was the first of Hui-neng's three principles of Zen, the other two being wu-hsin (formlessness) and wu-chu (non-abiding). Bodhidharma used wu-hsin (no-mind) with the same meaning as wu-nien (no-thought).

The principle of wu-nien is related to shūnyatā (emptiness), for the true self-nature is characterized by this, with reference to all else. It is also related to tathatā (suchness), for the self-nature cannot be known in terms of something else – 'I am what *I* am,' not what anything else is. This is the real depth-psychology.

Wu-wei. In Japanese, Mui. Non-action, or perhaps rather non-acting. Wu is identified with satori, in that when the satori comes there is in it no action – not even the action of thought, which is the action of the mind. Whether wu-wei leads to satori, or removes an obstacle to satori, or accompanies satori is a matter on which opinions differ and experience seems or may seem to differ. When it is said that in Chinese the word signifies satori, it really only means that satori *has* wu, or, in other words, it is used as an adjectival noun for the experience that is wu (or devoid of all form and action). There is in this an implication that one is talking of the samyak-sambuddhi (real experience) or the tao. Wu originated as a Taoist, not a Buddhist, term.

The use of the term Wu-wei as characterizing the Buddha-nature experience does not preclude the idea that mental activity with reference to material matters can be present along with the satori. Only in the seeking and finding and presence of satori there *must* be wu-wei; no sort of trance is implied.

This being so, the consciousness of the sage now consists of three ingredients, satori, mind and body, instead of merely two (the mind and body facts) as in the case of ordinary persons. When it is said that on the cessation of the sage's sansāra (*q.v.*) he is liberated, it means that mind and body are dropped and he is now 'in nirvāna'.

Y

Yang and Yin. The principles of the Yang and the Yin as presented in the system of Tao associated with the name of Lao-tsu are not denied by Zenists, but the aim of Zen is to realize the unity at the back of their duality. As far as thought operates in connection with these, it *doubts* the duality of the seeming pair, and so leads to tranquillity, which is a perception of the unity, not an inference that there must be unity.

To understand this one must know that Yang and Yin are names for the positive and negative principles in the world; life and matter, construction and preservation, male and female, etc. In Indian philosophy and tradition the two are regarded as the basic duality produced by thought, so that creation is the result of a fixed or directed thought, whether it be of a world by a God or any little thing by a man. It is, no doubt, the same fundamentally as the Logos doctrine of the Greeks and Christians, if we mean by Logos a spoken word, which is an affirmed thought, even a creative command.

The personalized expressions of these in the old Indian traditional stories (Purānas) are given as the Gods Vishnu and Brahmā, respectively Lord of Life and Lord of Creation, and as such responsible for 'time' and 'space', or, more accurately, process and form or extensity. In yoga philosophy, these conceptions are shown in dhāranā (concentration on a bhūmi, ground or object), dhyāna (meditation as a continuing process of thought) and samādhi (contemplation, which leads to realization of the truth behind the duality).

The old Chinese system of classification carried this distinction into almost everything, such as white and black, hardness and softness, happiness and sorrow, odd numbers and even numbers, even life and death and love and hate. The whole world was regarded as of contrasting pairs. These were, of course, contrasts, not negations; where there is contrast the two things must be of one kind. You cannot contrast an elephant with, let us say, the square root of two, but you can contrast it with a mouse, in point of size. Contrast always indicates a unity as the basis of every pair of opposites. In the *I Ching* system the two were indicated by one long dash (—) and two short ones or, rather, a divided line (--), respectively.

Yogāchāra School. See under Mahāyāna.

Yun-men. Ummon (*q.v.*).

122

Z

Zāzen. Meditation while sitting in the approved posture is called Zā-zen. It includes such matters as crossed legs, straight back, regular breathing, eyes only slightly open. It means sitting for a long time, and becoming calm. Some say that the sitting should be with the soles of the feet turned upwards, though not as in the 'lotus posture' (padmāsana) of the Hindus, in which the second foot comes up and between the calf and thigh of the other leg. (See also under Sesshin.)

Though the above remarks apply to the form of sitting in Zen monasteries in general, it should not be assumed that this is a necessary posture. One picture of a Zen Master shows him sitting on a hillside on a low rock with his legs stretched out in front partly bent at the knees. His back is by no means straight, but his face depicts the mental serenity of his mind. Bodhisattwas (*q.v.*) or Lohans are also sometimes depicted sitting on seats with one leg raised in front (as though cross-legged) and the other having the foot resting on the ground.

Hui-neng (*q.v.*), a great authority in this matter, had another explanation of his own. He said that when no thought arises in the mind it is called sitting (za) and to look at one's own nature inwardly is called meditation (Zen).

Zen. An abbreviation of the Japanese words Zenno and Zenna, derived from the Chinese word Ch'an (meditation), which in turn was derived from the Sanskrit word dhyāna.

The term is used both for the process of meditation and for its results in consciousness or, some would say, super-consciousness, meaning those states of consciousness which have no relation to the human personality-picture or self-image, and so are attainable only by eliminating the self-image for the time being. In this the self-without-image or self-beyond-image is to be realized.

Just as the memories of childhood are formed in relation to the self-image of the child, which develops slowly and becomes definite at the age of about four years, so the 'transcendental' experiences of the super-consciousness, though present in all, are not recognized by most people because they have no relation to the present self-image – they are not 'mine'. If, then, the present self-image can be recognized as false in the sense of not including the essential self-nature or even the bare experience of the consciousness named 'I', and then the meditation without false self-image can be continued, the result will be the realization of the true self-nature, with its included joy of freedom from dependencies.

This explanation of self-image is given here because the term has become so definite and so helpful in modern psychology and psychiatry, and quite clearly it plays a central part in producing the error of incompleteness of self-recognition in ordinary life. The use of this incompleteness in ordinary life is clear. It is to focus the mental attention on the business of bodily living. It has become a dominating habit, which the Zenist proposes to set aside voluntarily at special times by withdrawing into a special condition of meditation, a condition which at its best will become constantly present without special meditation or withdrawal. Thus the meditation practice and process are seen to be preparatory, just as physical setting-up exercises in the morning are intended to have their effects all through the day.

Zen has come to acquire a very special and exact meaning. It is no longer meditation in general, but meditation for this specific purpose of discovering or realizing the essential or real self-nature.

This specific system of meditation or school of thought reached Japan in the twelfth century, and became established in several somewhat differing sects. There are five well-known schools of Zen in Japan (see under Hui-neng) of which two are *strictly* zenic, having the specific purpose already explained. These two are the Rinzai (*q.v.*) and the Soto (*q.v.*).

Zen is described by Christmas Humphries, founder of the Buddhist Society (London), as 'the apotheosis of Buddhism', and a 'direct assault upon the citadel of Truth, without reliance upon concepts (of God or soul or salvation) or the use of scripture, ritual or vow'. It takes no scripture as authority.

In China, Zen is also called hsin-tsung, which means 'the teaching of the Mind', referring of course to the Buddha-mind, with its Enlightenment. This is really also the perfecting of the mind, for in the perfecting of the mind there is the discovery of the Buddha-mind. This is the very central and essential purpose of Zen Buddhism. The term mind is used as the equivalent of consciousness, and thus Zen becomes the pursuit of pure consciousness, not consciousness of *something* but of consciousness. The mind is concerned with both worldly and religious matters and so its study includes psychology, philosophy and religion, and so Zen must be regarded as scientific, philosophic and religious.

The three essentials for successful Zen have been given as (1) *Dai-shinkon*, great faith, (2) *Dai-gidan*, great doubt, and (3) *Dai-funshin*, great determination, which lead to Kensho-godo (*q.v.*). The essential means are meditation, inspiration and non-artificiality.

Zen and Philosophy. Dr D. T. Suzuki has pointed out that the tendency of many Zenists to avoid the study of scholastic Buddhism – as 'a pair of worn-out straw sandals' – led by the tenth century to a tendency among the more important to antinomianism and even to licentiousness. It has to be remembered that the meditator is still the imperfect man, and his ability to meditate will depend to a large extent upon his character and conduct. The 'freeness of the spirit' is one thing but the body must conform to nature. Licentiousness is not natural, but a disease of the human mind.

Zendo. Meditation Hall. In this the monks meditate and also sleep, each monk being allowed one mat space (3 ft by 6 ft). Here the monk lies down at night, using his one quilt and no pillow. The Hall is also used for sermons or lectures. (See under monasteries.)

Zen, Origin of. The form of Buddhism considered the most essential by Zenists is described as derived from a particular incident in the life of Buddha. When Buddha attained his illumination while sitting under the Bodhi tree at Gayā in India, the highest part of that attainment could not be given in verbal statements because it had no points of comparison with anything known or knowable to the senses (i.e. materials) or anything known or knowable to the mind (i.e., thoughts).

The incident in the life of Buddha which drew specific attention to the importance of the essential illumination and suggested a mode of looking by which this citadel was to be directly stormed – or this kingdom of heaven taken by force of meditation – occurred, according to the story, when Buddha held up a flower and looked at it. Seeing this, the disciple Mahākāshyapa smiled in a special way, for he had received the sudden enlightenment which came later to be called wu (in China) and satori (in Japan). Several Chinese texts, including *The Transmission of the Lamp* (Ching Te Ch'uan Teng Lu), state that Buddha spoke to Mahākāshyapa afterwards, giving the explanation as follows:

> The dharma's fundamental dharma has no dharma,
> The dharma of no-dharma is dharma too.
> Now that the dharma of no-dharma has been transmitted,
> Has there ever been a dharma?

Incidentally, this verse of Buddha's has been referred to as the first koan.

It is not denied by the Zenists that Buddha's illumination contained also a new explanation of life concerning the business of living among materials and thoughts – a new view and mode of life and mind – which he described in the Four Noble Truths. But it is held by them

125

that the teaching about body and mind which Buddha could and did thus give were and are inferior to the indescribable illumination which he also gave. It could be asserted that the new outlook given in the Four Noble Truths also arose from the essential illumination, in that the performance of this dhamma (or dharma), i.e. the way of life prescribed, while not strictly leading up to the zenic illumination, at least prepares the way for it by removing the obstacles to meditation which commonly clutter up human lives and minds.

In Buddha's time Hinduism for most people was a mass of do's and dont's (rules), somewhat as the conditions in early Judaism. This large collection of do's and dont's were in fact called in India the law or duty (dharma), and just as Jesus gave a new dispensation, replacing obedience by love, and saying that love of man and God would lead to the Father, so Buddha's Four Noble Truths were and are calculated to set a man on his own feet and release him from mere obedience. And just as Jesus said that all his daily life and teaching was only the carrying out of the Father's wishes, which he directly knew, so it could be said that Buddha's doctrine of the Four Noble Truths arose out of his essential and inexpressible illumination.

The difference between the Zenist and people of the other sects of Buddhism, then, is that he tries to give all his attention, or as much as he can of it, to meditation upon the essential fact of life, while the other people industriously pursue the Four Noble Truths, hoping that thereby the essential illumination will at some time somehow manifest itself in their consciousness. Some do both.

Three essentials for successful Zen, entirely in line with Bodhidharma's promotion of it, no doubt have been given as (1) great faith (dai-shinko), (2) great doubt (dai-gidan), and (3) great determination (dai-funshin), which lead to kensho-godo (q.v.).

Zen, The Word. Zen is an abbreviated form of the words zenna and zenjo, which came from the Chinese Ch'an and channa, which again were from the Sanskrit dhyāna, and its form jhana in the Pali language (which Buddha spoke).

Dhyāna is translated as meditation, which is well defined by Patanjali as a continued flow of ideation, but in the strict schools of Zen in China and Japan, and in their recent extensions into the Western world, Zen is understood as going beyond thought into the condition of poise called samādhi (often translated as contemplation) in Sanskrit. The word dhyāna is still commonly used in India in a general way to cover all forms of concentration, meditation and contemplation. The strictness of the term in the Meditation Schools of China and Japan derives from its definition by Bodhidharma.

Zen, Three Requirements for. Great faith, great doubt and great perseverance. The second of these does not go against the first, because it refers to the problems of self and life. The third can be taken as courage, as well as persistence in the face of repeated failure. The last is helped by the knowledge that the Satori may come suddenly through an unexpected sense-perception, perhaps on hearing right into a bird's song, or seeing right into something, right to the Buddha-nature in that.

Select Bibliography

Blofeld, John (trans.), *Zen Teaching of Huang-Po*, The Buddhist Society, London, 1968

Blofeld, John (trans.), *Zen Teaching of Hui Hai*, Rider, 1970

Blyth, R. H., *Zen and Zen Classics*, 5 vols, Japan Publications, San Francisco: vol. 1, 1964; vol. 2, 1964; vol. 3, 1970; vol. 4, 1966; vol. 5, 1972

Herrigel, E., *The Method of Zen*, Routledge, 1960

Herrigel, E., *Zen in the Art of Archery*, Routledge, 1972

Humphreys, Christmas, *Zen Buddhism*, Allen & Unwin, 1962

Humphreys, Christmas, *Western Approach to Zen*, Allen & Unwin, 1972

Hyers, M. Conrad, *Zen and the Comic Spirit*, Rider, 1974

K'Uo-an, *Ox and his Herdsman: A Chinese Zen Text*, trans. M. Trevor, International Publications Service, New York, 1969

Leggett, Trevor, *A First Zen Reader*, Tuttle, Tokyo, 1960 (UK distributor: International Book Distributors Ltd)

Luk, Charles, *Ch'an and Zen Teachings*, 3 vols, Rider, 1960–62

Masunaga, R., *Primer of Soto Zen*, Routledge, 1972

Reps, Paul, *Zen Flesh, Zen Bones*, Penguin, 1971

Schloegl, Irmgard, *Record of Rinzai*, The Buddhist Society, London, 1975

Schloegl, Irmgard, *The Wisdom of the Zen Masters*, Sheldon Press, London, 1975

Suzuki, D. T., *The Field of Zen*, The Buddhist Society, London, 1969

Suzuki, D. T., *Introduction to Zen Buddhism*, Rider, 1969

Suzuki, D. T., *The Zen Doctrine of No Mind*, Rider, 1969

Suzuki, D. T., *Essays in Zen Buddhism*, 3 vols, Rider, 1970

Suzuki, D. T., *Manual of Zen Buddhism*, Rider, 1973

Suzuki, S., *Zen Mind, Beginner's Mind*, Weatherhill, New York, 1972; paperback, 1973 (U.K. distributor: Phaidon)

Uchiyama, Kosho, *Approach to Zen: The Reality of Zazen*, Japan Publications, San Francisco, 1974

Watts, Alan, *The Way of Zen*, Penguin, 1970

Watts, Alan, *The Spirit of Zen*, John Murray, 1972

Wetering, J. Van De, *The Empty Mirror: Experiences in a Japanese Zen Monastery*, Routledge, 1973

Wong Mou-dam (trans.), *The Sutra of Hui Neng*, The Buddhist Society, London, 1966

57 L